Praise for
Intentional Success

The insights in *Intentional Success* for running a successful business are priceless.

Chris Widener
New York Times bestselling author

Everyone who dreams of starting their own business will benefit from the step-by-step leadership instructions in this book.

Hal Elrod
Author of *The Miracle Morning*

If you want to go beyond ordinary to achieve the extraordinary read this book! Brad Taylor's indispensable wisdom will unlock your potential and help you reach the entrepreneurial goals you dream of achieving.

Roger Crawford
Bestselling author and host of Motivational Mondays with Roger Crawford on The Tennis Channel

Intentional Success, I love this title and it fits! Brad Taylor does an outstanding job of sharing the power of entrepreneurship and teaching how to build a successful small business! Full of practical, usable, and proven advice, it's a quick, easy read comprising both instruction and interesting and relevant stories and examples.

Tom Ziglar
CEO of Ziglar, Inc. Proud son of Zig Ziglar

Brad Taylor has tremendous success in business, yet his transparent writing on learning from failures makes this book hard to set aside. A must read business book.

Patricia Fripp
CSP, CPAE, award-winning keynote speaker, author

Great example of not letting others get in your way of pursuing your dreams.

Rudy Ruettiger
Author, motivational speaker, inspiration behind the film Rudy

INTENTIONAL SUCCESS

THE POWER OF ENTREPRENEURSHIP

BRAD TAYLOR

Made for Success
PUBLISHING

Made For Success Publishing
P.O. Box 1775 Issaquah, WA 98027
www.MadeForSuccessPublishing.com

Distributed by Made for Success Publishing

Library of Congress Cataloging-in-Publication data

Taylor, Brad
Intentional Success: The Power of Entrepreneurship
p. cm.

ISBN: 978-1-64146-314-0 (HDBK)
ISBN: 978-1-64146-347-8 (PBK)
ISBN: 978-1-64146-315-7 (eBOOK)
LCCN: 2018945960

This book is dedicated to all the individuals who have inspired me throughout my life; most importantly my wife, my children, and my family.

-Brad Taylor

CONTENTS

Foreword. ix

Introduction xi

Chapter 1: Intangibles of Success 1

Chapter 2: How the Journey Began 25

Chapter 3: Risking It All to Succeed. 33

Chapter 4: Persistence in Sales 41

Chapter 5: Time Management & Goal Setting. 61

Chapter 6: Struggles & Lessons Learned. 71

Chapter 7: Working with Your Spouse 91

Chapter 8: Sustainability 101

Chapter 9: Importance of Leadership. 127

Chapter 10: True International Success. 139

About the Author. 151

FOREWORD

BRAD TAYLOR IS passion.

I remember talking with Brad about my new business venture like it was yesterday. He was so passionate you could feel every word he spoke through the phone. I loved talking with Brad. He is a mentor, friend, and a person I truly look up to.

Passion, aka "I pass on," is just what he did for my family and me. When Brad and I met, I was a teacher. I loved teaching, but I knew there were other things that I could do. Being an entrepreneur was not one of them, or so I thought.

It didn't take long for me to begin to see the world through Brad's eyes. He has the ability to transfer passion to others, and I am confident that you too will feel his passion as you read this book and learn the twelve intangibles of success.

I know the foreword is not usually the place to thank the author, but I'm not going to go the usual route.

Brad, thank you! Thank you for changing my life and helping me find my passion.

My family and I are forever changed because of you and your amazing wife, Cathy.

Thank you for answering my calls at all times of the day and walking me through the entrepreneurial hurdles as I began my business over seven years ago.

I remember calling you when my first magazine was printed. I sat in my garage in tears thinking about all the hard work I put in. I was filled with joy and awe.

Thank you for helping me understand the importance of passion and how it brings joy to others as well as myself.

It is an honor to work with you, Brad. But the greatest honor I can say is knowing you are a friend and a mentor.

Thank You!

Tomas Martinez III
Business Coach and Speaker
Publisher/Owner of LHM Austin-San Antonio, TX

INTRODUCTION

WHAT DOES "INTENTIONAL SUCCESS" mean?

Intentional success is about making choices to take positive steps that will make a difference throughout your entire life, from this day on, moving forward.

Everyone faces difficult decisions every day. It's the decisions you choose to make that will dictate how your personal, professional and family life will be defined, evaluated, characterized and altered.

in•ten•tion•al

adjective: intentional—done on purpose; deliberate.

If you've been in the business world in any capacity, for any length of time, you've probably realized that success doesn't come by accident. True success comes from careful planning (intentional planning), patience, hard work, hustling, learning, discipline, taking calculated risks, being humble and having a devotion to seeing your dreams and goals come to fruition.

My wife, Cathy, and I have been intentional every step of the way through our professional and personal lives. We made an intentional and deliberate decision to move our entire lives across the country to pursue our dreams, to believe in the "intangibles of success," lead by example in every aspect of our lives and run our business with transparency and integrity.

But most importantly, we have been intentional in helping other people succeed in seeing their dreams realized.

The book you have in your hands is for the aspiring entrepreneur, the business professional, the dreamer, and the doer. You will discover tools, practical applications and real-life examples of what intentional success looks like—in both your professional and personal life. Whatever industry you are in—whether it's sales, hospitality, the service sector, the medical field, the arts or education—there is something to be taken from this book that can be applied to every single area of your life.

The twelve intangibles—attributes and traits consistently referenced throughout the chapters—are the blueprint you need to guide your professional career. The twelve intangibles will help you run your business, manage your employees, be an effective leader and grow your organization to the next level, regardless of the type of business or industry you are in.

This blueprint is what prepares you to intentionally succeed and position yourself to win in anything you set out to achieve.

1 INTANGIBLES OF SUCCESS

"Being challenged in life is inevitable, being defeated is optional."

-Roger Crawford

THERE ARE TWELVE "intangibles" that create the foundation for establishing overall success, both in business and in your daily life.

Intangibles are qualities you can't necessarily touch—they have no physical presence. They are the qualities—one's persona, self-insight, presence, fortitude, values, characteristics, traits, skills, and behaviors—that make up the foundation for being a respected executive, an incredible leader and a highly successful entrepreneur.

The intangibles of success outlined in this chapter are not listed in any specific order. Each of the twelve is equally important in truly defining your character while giving you the strategic principles to gain insight, grow as a person and pursue anything you set out to accomplish.

I have heard many people from all walks of life reference the word "intangibles" regarding specific topics, but never as described throughout this book.

"If you can dream it, you can do it."

-Walt Disney

TWELVE INTANGIBLES
OF SUCCESS

FAITH
SPIRITUALITY

BELIEF
FEAR

PASSION
ATTITUDE

POSTURE
CONFIDENCE

EMPATHY
COMPASSION

RELATABILITY
COMMUNICATION

PERSISTENCE
CONSISTENCY

INTEGRITY
CHARACTER

KNOWLEDGE
WISDOM

GOALS
INTENTIONS

LEADERSHIP
VISION

BALANCE
RECHARGE

1. FAITH | SPIRITUALITY

I believe that, in many ways, faith is what keeps you grounded and accountable regarding your actions and the way we intentionally live our daily lives—both at work and home.

"Now faith is confidence in what we hope for and assurance about what we do not see" (Hebrews 11:1).

Faith also forces you to reassess your priorities, successes, and failures in life on a consistent basis.

Ultimately, faith is what gets you through the struggles, challenges, and adversities you face day-in and day-out. For my wife and I, faith has always been an important part of our marriage, family and how we have operated our businesses.

Faith has allowed us to get through trying times in business, with the passing of loved ones in our family and in raising our children.

Personally, I'm not embarrassed about my faith and let others around me know my involvement in the church we attend—but never push my religion on anyone.

I am proud to have faith as one of the intangibles of success.

> **Without GOD, life has no purpose, and without purpose, life has no meaning. Without meaning, life has no significance or hope."**
> -Rick Warren

2. **BELIEF** | FEAR

Believing in yourself is vital to achieving your dreams. Unfortunately, belief is an obstacle most individuals struggle with throughout their entire lives. Belief stems from the reason you're doing what you're doing. However, you must first understand your purpose in creating the why, both in your personal and professional life.

> "Taking a chance is better than regretting you never tried."

Belief alone is not enough to achieve your ultimate dreams unless you incorporate the other eleven intangibles outlined in this chapter.

As the saying goes, "Let your dreams be bigger than your fears." Most of us can attest to the fact that there is always a little voice in our heads telling us that we can't do what we really want to do in life. We tell ourselves things like: it's not the right time; I'm too young; I'm too old; I don't have enough experience; I'm crazy to think this could work; I don't deserve success, etc. Oftentimes, there is both an internal negative voice and a person or people in our lives telling us that we will never be able to accomplish our dreams or goals. In the case of another person discouraging us, sometimes it is because the person does not believe we have the impetus or motivation to achieve our goals, or that we are on the right career path for success. Sometimes it is because the other person is projecting his or her fears and self-doubt on us. Whatever motivates it, their attacks on us and our aspirations create doubt, which at the end of the day, kill more dreams than failure ever will.

Have you ever had something in life you really wanted to pursue? Is there something that meant so much to you that you used to think about it all the time, day after day, week after week— but you never really did anything about it? As time has passed and your life has moved forward, have you ever looked back and wondered: "What if? What if I had chosen to commit to this goal or dream and follow through with intention? Would it have changed my life? Would it have changed my family's life? Will I look back at the end of my life and regret that I didn't take that risk? Have I missed out on the chance to create financial stability for my family by not taking that leap of faith? How much have I lost, how much have I missed out on by not pursuing my dreams?"

"Belief is what gives you hope, strength and the courage to change."

In Chapter Three, I write about a time in the early 1990s when my wife and I decided to move from Florida to Oregon to pursue a new business opportunity. We believed that this was the right career path for us, even though we were told point blank, multiple times before leaving Florida, that we were making a colossal mistake, were destined to fail and would be right back where we started within the year.

> "People regret decisions they should have made in their life because they listened to their friends, neighbors, family and naysayers instead of taking that risk to pursue their dreams."

Understanding there were going to be challenges, sacrifices and disappointments along the way, we had the belief that we were going to succeed—regardless of what obstacles we might face. If we didn't try, we would never know whether true success was possible.

As I made two trips between Florida and Oregon over the next few months, driving both of our vehicles over 3,100 miles, belief is what kept me going, what kept me focused, what kept me committed and what kept me on track. I know this to be true because our why was our purpose and motivation in overcoming any barriers we would encounter throughout our journey.

As I look back, I think my biggest concerns at the time were all the unknowns in starting a new business venture across the country, far away from our family, my kids and our friends. We were moving to a new city—Portland—where we didn't know a single soul.

> "Whatever drives you will inspire you to be the very best in whatever you set out to accomplish."

As I mentor professionals and entrepreneurs today, it has become clear that not everyone has that belief in what they are pursuing—neither in their business nor their personal lives.

Part of being a true entrepreneur is having the unconditional belief that you will be successful in whatever business venture you pursue. More importantly, you must have a burning desire to succeed, to be all in, knowing it's the belief that will ultimately bring you real success in whatever you set out to accomplish.

> "If you really want to do something,
> you'll find a way. If you don't,
> you'll find an excuse."
>
> *-Jim Rohn*

3. **PASSION** | ATTITUDE

Being passionate about the things you are choosing to pursue is a large part of what will motivate and drive you every day to succeed.

Passion and enthusiasm are incredibly contagious, as everyone wants to be around individuals with a positive, uplifting, excitable and infectious attitude.

But passion and enthusiasm cannot be taught. Just like you don't "learn to love" someone, you don't "learn to have passion." Passion is like energy. You can't teach energy. But you can cultivate and harness energy, and you can do the same with passion and enthusiasm.

Think about the last person you were around that was really passionate about something or enthusiastic. Did it impact your enthusiasm?

Passion, enthusiasm, and attitude play a huge part in how you will achieve your ultimate goals, as well as how people will perceive you.

> ## "Nothing great was ever achieved without enthusiasm."
> *-Ralph Waldo Emerson*

When you love what you are doing, everyone wants to be part of it. Passion radiates from your expressions, conversations, actions, emotion, body language, charisma, and enthusiasm—regardless of what it is in response to.

Having a great attitude and being passionate about what you are doing is what makes everyone around you feel better about themselves and their purpose, as well as fostering excitement about life in general.

> ## "Your passion needs to be bigger than your fear in order to succeed."

As I say just about every week to someone, your ATTITUDE in life is EVERYTHING and will dictate your overall ambition to succeed. When you hang around negative people you will become more negative—and their destructive attitude will tear you down over time.

When you surround yourself with uplifting, positive dreamers, doers, believers and inspirational individuals looking to lift you up, you'll be filled with an awesome attitude and an amazing outlook about life in general.

Your passion is part of who you are already, passion has purpose and meaning. You can't share your passion with others until you find passion within yourself.

Find your passion, discover your purpose and you will understand your meaning in life.

> "It's your attitude, more than your aptitude, that will determine your altitude."
>
> -Zig Ziglar

4. POSTURE | CONFIDENCE

In the business world, having a confident stance in how you present and represent yourself allows your colleagues, clients, business associates and the individuals you interact with on a consistent basis to take you seriously.

Posture—the way we present ourselves—is not enough without confidence, as confidence gives you the feeling of self-assurance. In fact, it's critical that posture and confidence are expressed equally through your actions and interactions with others.

One who does not possess this quality will likely struggle in any professional setting.

Having a lack of confidence and posture is often indicated through body language, poor communication skills, choice of language or wording, mannerisms, and even unconscious gestures.

Posture allows you to lose all the excuses and focus solely on your confidence."

I also firmly believe that your appearance will directly reflect your posture in business—not to mention the other eleven intangibles.

If you're dressed professionally (based on the industry you are in), you will feel more confident, which will impact your attitude, disposition, and self-esteem.

Perception and first impressions are everything."

In the book "It's Your Move," by Josh Altman, he makes a great analogy about the importance of dressing appropriately: your dress is your uniform for your job, so wear it proudly and professionally.

Posture also involves how you greet someone and introduce yourself. Make sure you make eye contact, shake their hand firmly as you introduce yourself, and smile—nobody wants to look at someone with a frown. Personally, I am one of those guys that will hold both your hands when I shake to say good-bye. I want the person I have just spent time with to understand that I highly value them. It instills that you care about them and about the conversation that you just had and that you are looking forward to following up and interacting with them soon.

Lastly, keep your phone out of sight with the ringer on silent, NOT in your hand, as you are having a conversation, in a meeting or giving a presentation. You're not there to be on your phone;

you're there to give the person or individuals you are interacting with your total, undivided attention.

> When you have confidence in yourself,
> others will gain confidence in you."

5. **EMPATHY** | COMPASSION

Empathy is the ability to understand, care and honestly express your sincere feelings to others. In many ways, empathy and relatability—also among the intangibles—are similar but have two different meanings.

> Empathy is truly caring and
> communicating from your heart while
> being compassionate, having patience,
> humility and listening with sincerity."

People want to know you care about them, have their best interests in mind, and that you acknowledge their accomplishments. They don't want to be treated like a number in the system, which will be discussed in multiple chapters throughout this book.

Empathy is not just used with your team or employees who represent you. If you are in sales, you will need to use empathy with your clients. If you are in the teaching profession, your students will benefit from empathy. If you are in the hospitality or service industry, your guests or customers will benefit from empathy. If you are in the medical field, empathy will go a long way with your patients.

People want to be associated with a company where empathy is part of the culture, is representative of the everyday actions of the organization—as empathy brings out the best in morale and shows true caring for both the industry and the individual.

6. **RELATABILITY** | COMMUNICATION

Relatability is the ability to connect and read people while being able to listen to their needs and be attentive to their thoughts, concerns, ideas, and suggestions.

Relatability could be a chapter in and of itself, as it encompasses the skills of communication, clarity, collaboration, engagement, friendliness, influence and respect. I spend a lot of time talking about this very subject.

It took me years to master the art of relatability, and it's something I now know is my biggest weakness. When someone is telling a story that I can relate to, I would often accidentally interrupt and start to share my own personal experiences while they were still telling their story.

Have you ever done this before?

My wife would always, or should I say still, corrects me by saying; "Brad, it's not about you," which translates to:

"Brad, it's not about you and your stories; it's about them and their experiences in the stories they are sharing."

You see, it's human nature to talk about ourselves and our experiences, but it takes skill and a LOT of practice to LISTEN with both ears. Make sure that when you choose to speak, you are not making the conversation about yourself, but about the person you are interacting with.

If you dominate the conversation, or worse yet, consistently interrupt the person talking, they will soon feel you are not interested in what they are saying. They will likely get the impression that what they are saying is not important to you and will ultimately tune you out of the conversation altogether.

The skill of intently listening applies not only to business but in your own personal life: with your spouse, significant other, children, extended family, events you attend and friends you associate with.

Today, because of the rise of technology, relatability can be compromised due to not having the confidence, courage, communication and social skills in building solid relationships in person. We have often built relationships through the facade of social media, email, and texting, which will never build true, solid, transparent relationships structured on the foundation of trust, integrity, and credibility.

7. PERSISTENCE | CONSISTENCY

If I had to pick just one word that defined being successful in business, I would say it would be PERSISTENCE—without question!

In my opinion, it is persistence combined with consistency that creates the action, activity, credibility, and results each time a defined, measurable goal is set.

Persistence also inspires others to see your commitment, drive, and fortitude to hold on and get back up when struggles may knock you down and challenge you.

I have dedicated a chapter later in this book to the topic of "persistence in sales," so I won't elaborate too much. I will say, it's persistence and the other eleven intangibles that define your drive, tenacity, determination, courage, perseverance and overall burning desire to never give up in whatever you set out to do—regardless if it's a short-term or long-term goal.

8. INTEGRITY | CHARACTER

To me, integrity is everything. Knowing that you are doing the right thing, even when no one is looking, is what sets you apart from all the others.

I am a big believer in being transparent when running a business, as transparency forces you to consistently be truthful, honest, sincere and accountable when creating and capturing value in the product, brand or services you represent or provide.

> **The easiest thing to sell is ALWAYS the truth."**

Integrity is also exhibited in leading by example, and not asking someone to do something you're not willing to do yourself. Integrity involves treating EVERYONE the way you would want to be treated—regardless of their status, education, profession, current situation or upbringing.

Don't pretend to be someone you're not in life, even when placed in uncomfortable surroundings. Integrity is based on being who you are and saying what you mean. Be sure you are not promising something you have NO intention of ever acting on or fulfilling.

> Your WORD should mean
> everything in business."

But, at the end of the day, it's your character, trust, credibility, actions, emotions, selflessness, moral principles, values, work ethic and authenticity that define your integrity in life.

> Never trade integrity and respect
> for attention, ever!"

9. KNOWLEDGE | WISDOM

Your greatest competitive advantage is knowledge. When I think of knowledge in business, I view it in three segments:

(1) Wisdom/Maturity

(2) Research and

(3) Investing in Yourself.

1. Wisdom/Maturity

Learning from your mistakes allows you to grow as a person.

It teaches you humility in your daily actions while causing you to reflect on what you could have done differently.

This forces you to not simply assess what just happened but take full responsibility for it (which is extremely hard for most individuals). You can choose to walk in wisdom by reflecting on why the situation happened, who was affected, what you learned from the experience and how to change the situation, so it doesn't happen again. Successful leaders learn from their setbacks—which ultimately become some of their greatest learning lessons.

> ## Your best teacher is the last mistake you made."

2. Research

Knowing your industry and the surroundings related to your business or field is critically important to the success of the product, brand, service or profession you represent.

It's amazing how many professionals represent an industry they know very little about or don't take the time to understand thoroughly. To me, understanding your competition and their weaknesses is a given, yet many don't take this seriously, leaving themselves or their business extremely vulnerable.

It's not what you are doing today, next month or even next year. It's what you will be doing five years from now that will differentiate you, your brand and your business from others.

This basic principle also applies in sales and targeting your potential customers, audience and the general demographic you are trying to capture.

> **Doing your research is doing your homework on who you are targeting and completely understanding your customers' needs."**

Years ago, people used to joke that I was stalking my prospects, but what I was doing was making sure I knew everything about the person or company I would be contacting—putting me in a better position than anyone else.

If you do your research correctly, you will be amazed by the outcome of your presentation. I can't imagine giving a presentation without completely understanding everything about the person or company I am targeting, but too many do just that in sales alone.

The best presentations of products and services are built around the knowledge (homework) and research of the person or company you are pitching to.

> **Preparation and Research makes up 90% of the Presentation."**

This allows you to not only create the need and unique value, but it demonstrates your willingness to take the time to completely understand their company, weaknesses, strengths, goals and long-term objectives.

To this day, it amazes me how many calls I get wanting to

sell me something, yet the person calling me doesn't know a thing about what I do or the type of business I have.

3. Investing in yourself

I have been reading motivational books and listening to inspirational speakers on audio for over 30+ years, always learning something from each one.

To be successful as an entrepreneur or leader of a company or organization, you will need to be willing to invest in yourself, be humble and learn from others.

> **Develop a burning desire to learn, and you will grow beyond your wildest expectation."**

When my wife and I first arrived in Portland, Oregon in the early '90s, the first year was tough—no, it was incredibly brutal. My wife and I didn't know anyone, and we were just starting up our company. It felt like we were all alone; thousands of miles away from all our family and friends.

I contribute a considerable part of the success of launching our first several magazine titles in the early '90s, and the continued growth we had moving forward, to listening to motivational speakers like Les Brown. Les and a variety of other speakers were in my car, keeping me motivated day after day, bringing me inspiration when I was down, and giving me high-fives when things were going great. I couldn't get enough of these motivational speakers' audio cassette tapes to listen to as I drove from appointment to appointment.

> **"Not all readers are leaders, but all leaders are readers."**
>
> *-Harry S. Truman*

These speakers gave me the inspiration to succeed and to keep moving on, regardless of the struggles, challenges, and obstacles I faced. I not only related to their stories but loved the examples that were shared of their own personal lives—all with inspirational messages and quotes along the way. It was like these speakers were part of my daily life.

> **"Today, being AVERAGE is NOT enough to truly succeed."**

Regardless of the industry you are in—or if it's just to motivate yourself personally to accomplish a specific goal in life—consistently reading and listening to positive motivational stories is the best therapy you will ever receive. There are now thousands of motivational posts, audio, podcasts, and video to relate to and download using the internet and social media.

In my office, I have hundreds of books and audio on the history of companies, entrepreneurs, speakers, CEOs, etc. As I talk with professionals, I am continually sharing them based on the topic, challenge or struggle they may be having. For me, as great as it is having a digital version of a book to view on your tablet or mobile device, there is nothing like reading a physical book. Nothing beats holding a book in your hands while making notes on a specific page or highlighting a paragraph you could really relate to, then sharing that book with someone. But if you can't do that, listen to the book on audio as you travel, drive, have quiet time or just work out.

10. **GOALS** | INTENTIONS

I have dedicated a chapter in this book on the importance of (1) time management, (2) ten strategic principles that will allow you to tackle any goal you set out to accomplish and (3) visual goal setting. All are vitally important in allowing you to stay organized, focused, leverage your time and follow through on the execution of the tasks and goals you set out to achieve.

> "Setting goals is forcing you NOT to be in the same place, this time, next year."

Regardless of the technology out there today, visual goal setting is one of the most powerful exercises you can do, regardless of your learning style. When you create a vision board or have visuals of specific tasks or goals you want to accomplish placed in front of you constantly, you end up doing short visualization exercises throughout the day.

This allows you to be accountable, focused on your intentions and actions and gives you clarity and reinforcement on specific goals. Athletes, for example, have utilized visual goal setting and vision boards for decades to strategically improve their overall performance standards.

Goals are not only absolutely necessary
to motivate us, but they are also
essential to really keep us alive."

-*Robert H. Schuller*

11. LEADERSHIP | VISION

I love the saying, "True leaders don't create more followers, they create more leaders." To me, leadership needs to come from your heart; it is something you need to earn, and should never, ever be taken for granted nor expected.

A great leader's courage to fulfill his vision
comes from PASSION, not position."

-*John Maxwell*

I am constantly asked why I still have a passion for what I do, and what keeps me going every day. This question can be answered in multiple ways, but I think it starts by having the love, willingness, clarity, vision and drive to inspire others to succeed while truly caring about ones' overall success intentionally.

Your organization is only as
good as the leadership."

Leadership is being a servant leader, all while:

1. Allowing you to focus on significance rather than success

2. Commitment to helping others grow, get out of their comfort zone and dream more

3. Focusing on purpose rather than just numbers

4. Listening intently, asking lots of questions, observing closely and never, never making assumptions

5. Encouraging others rather than micromanaging others

6. Leading by example.

12. **BALANCE** I RECHARGE

Taking care of oneself is vitally important, yet it is a constant struggle to balance everything we are trying to accomplish.

Regardless of the responsibilities, you may have, and what you do as a profession, everyone needs to recharge themselves on a regular basis. Stress affects the other eleven intangibles of success outlined in this chapter, not to mention your marriage, co-workers, friends and family life as well.

Everyone has a different way to deal with stress, relax, recharge, reenergize themselves and bring clarity to issues they may be challenged by or struggling within both their personal and professional lives. This can be broken down into the following five segments.

1. For some, working out—regardless if it's going to the gym, yoga, running, walking, boxing, biking, etc.—is therapeutic. Not to mention it keeps your body in shape as you deal with

the daily grind. For others, it's having a hobby, working in the yard, reading, fishing, water sports, golfing, etc.

2. Many look forward to getting away for a few days to clear their minds every so often. This could involve going camping, hiking, skiing, or taking a short trip to explore new areas while creating memories along the way.

3. Finding a balance between work and family while understanding your priorities and learning how to balance them is critical to being intentionally successful. This is truly positioning yourself to win.

With that said, there must be an understanding that when you make a commitment to be an entrepreneur, business owner or take on a larger management role within your company, there are going to be sacrifices you will need to address with your family along the way.

You need to talk to your family, so they understand that the rewards during your journey will most likely be down the road; not instantaneous. This process also creates enormous value for your family as they understand and appreciate your hard work and sacrifice. More importantly, they will appreciate the quality time you spend with them—and the rewards you reap throughout your journey of success.

4. It's also important to have open communication with your spouse or significant other when you don't work together. Remember: they can't read your mind. This process allows both of you to understand what may be happening at work, as well as issues that may come up that occasionally

take you away from family, friends and, activities you otherwise may have attended.

5. Lastly, it's imperative you take time out of your busy schedule to spend quality time with your kids, spouse or significant other. That means NOT using your cell phone when you are together, on a date, out to dinner, at the park, going to the movies or just taking a walk together. Quality time means just that—giving each other your total, undivided attention.

> "Be in the moment... Live in the moment... Enjoy the moment..."
>
> *-Brandy T. McCormack*

If you are a business owner, you can't do everything yourself. If you try, it's only a matter of time before you ultimately burn yourself out and lose your passion—not to mention the drive that pushed you to become the entrepreneur you are today.

2 HOW THE JOURNEY BEGAN

"Never ask someone to do something you're not willing to do yourself."

en•tre•pre•neur

noun: one who organizes, manages and assumes the risk of a business or enterprise.

EVER SINCE I can remember, I have always had the dream—or should I say burning desire—of being an entrepreneur, even before I could spell the word or knew what it truly meant.

My first experience of entrepreneurship was spending time with my grandfather, who owned his own plumbing business. I really enjoyed working and spending time with him during my summers as a young child. All his clients loved him, his business was totally built on referrals, and he stayed tremendously busy maintaining clients even after retiring—right up until his passing.

My second experience was when I was 13, maintaining two paper routes with the Cleveland Press after I came home from school. There, I quickly learned the responsibility of collecting money from the homeowners I delivered to, paying the route driver, and keeping my percentage; always entering whatever sales contest they introduced and winning as many contests as I could. I also understood at an early age that holding a job required a commitment, regardless of the weather, and boy did we have challenging weather in Cleveland during the winter. I also got my first taste of customer service—which, of course, came with customer complaints as well—while delivering the paper on my bike to over 60 homes, six days a week in a spread-out, rural suburb of Ohio.

During that time, I also started a landscaping business, borrowing my dad's tractor to cut grass and pick up leaves in our neighborhood. I learned to market and brand myself through flyers I designed to grow my business, while still delivering the newspaper. I was hungry to make money and learn about business. I loved reading about successful entrepreneurs, inventors, and business at the school library; dreaming of the opportunity to one day own my own business.

I couldn't wait until I was 16 to get my first job working for a home improvement store called Forest City Home Improvements, where I was placed in the garden center selling lawn mowers and tractors. During the summer of my high school graduation, one of my co-workers said there was a mega drug store that just opened down the street called Bernie Shulman's, and they were accepting applications for full-time employment. I applied for and got my first full-time position.

It was a huge 35,000+ square foot operation, which incorporated retail and a massive warehouse to hold all the inventory that was purchased with deals the manufacturers offered.

This inventory would then be stocked in the retail space daily due to the volume of merchandise sold. The retail portion of the store was incredible—with 12 to 15 cash registers being operated at any one time, all the time, from opening to closing, seven days a week. It was like nothing I had ever seen before.

I was so excited to get my first full-time job there, starting in the warehouse unloading trucks and checking in the shipments that were received off the purchase orders written.

For the next two years, I worked full-time at Shulman's, part-time at Forest City and took business classes at the college. Unfortunately, I just couldn't see myself going to college full time; I was more driven and focused on just making money and figuring out what I was going to do in life.

Over the next twelve years, I worked my way up from the warehouse to warehouse manager, buyer, general manager of the Mayfield Heights, OH location (until it was purchased by another chain called Marc's in 1983), to co-owner of Terry Shulman's located in Sarasota, Florida. (I ended up selling my interest in that location in 1987.)

I loved working at Shulman's, but more importantly, it introduced me to the world of retail, marketing, advertising, purchasing, management, start-up and overall operations of running a retail business. Working there, I was inspired by both owners, which significantly impacted my drive to be an entrepreneur. They taught me how important your work ethic is and how it will impact the people around you—something I talk about throughout this book and the learning lessons I use to coach and mentor entrepreneurs all over the country today.

The Shulmans weren't new to retail, as Bernie Shulman was the pioneer of the retail drug industry. Previously, Bernie Shulman was the founder of one of the most successful and largest drug store chains in the late '50s and early '60s called Revco Drug Store. Shulman took Revco public in 1964, and in 1966, he retired from Revco. In 1975, Bernie and Terry Shulman came out of retirement, introducing a totally new mega-discount drug store format in Mayfield Heights, Ohio called Bernie Shulman's Drug Store. This store was once estimated by the Wall Street Journal in the mid-80s to have the highest sales of any single drugstore location in the United States.

Several months after starting work at Shulman's, I was put in charge of managing the logistics of the warehouse. Due to the quantity of inventory that was received daily—based on the deals purchased from the manufacturers—it would be nothing to have four to five semi-trucks waiting to be unloaded at any one time.

Bernie Shulman was a registered pharmacist and would frequently come into the warehouse just about the same time every day around noon. He was always dressed professionally, wearing a white shirt and a tie.

I didn't know what to think of it—why was one of the owners hanging out in the hot (or during the winter extremely cold) warehouse with me in a tie?

He would use the time to ask me questions about myself, and always listened very attentively to my answers. I knew he was paying attention because the next day he would continue the conversation where we left off.

Bernie would ask me about my goals, dreams, parents, siblings, and what drew me to work at their store. He was always inquisitive, yet very positive. I can remember many times after unloading several pallets off a truck and checking in the merchandise; he would ask, "What can I do to help?" He would go on to start reading off the item numbers of the merchandise as I would check it off against the purchase orders written, placing the boxes on the rollers that would take the inventory to specific locations throughout the warehouse. He really did care, which at first, I thought was so unusual. Why would a very successful business owner take time out of the pharmacy and spend it with an 18-year-old kid unloading trucks in the warehouse?

Mr. Shulman even started bringing me lunch after a while—a corned beef sandwich. After a week or so, one day he asked me, "You're not eating the whole sandwich, don't you like corned beef?" The funny thing was, I was so intimidated by him at first that I was afraid to tell him otherwise! But he soon caught on and started bringing me ham and cheese instead.

I soon saw a different side of Bernie Shulman that was filled with sincerity, compassion and lots of humor—he always had a joke to tell. After several months, we even started going to lunch together every other Friday. I remember nervously commenting, "We can't be gone long, I'm going to have trucks waiting to be unloaded." Mr. Shulman responded by saying, "You've earned time to get away every other week with the boss. So, moving forward, don't schedule any trucks every other Friday between noon and one."

This became a lesson for me in being successful in business—which I would continue to utilize in all my business ventures moving forward. It all started with a series of words or phrases I would describe as being effective in business listening. That is exactly what Bernie Shulman did—listen.

Terry Shulman, Bernie's wife, would go on to become what I would consider my first true business mentor. Mrs. Shulman was always dressed professionally and taught me that you should never ask someone to do something you're not willing to do yourself, among many other things. She always led by example for others to follow.

Mrs. Shulman would often be working in the office one moment, then operating a cash register the next when things became incredibly busy, or stocking shelves with the latest shipment of hair coloring or vitamins that had just arrived.

She was tough but very fair. She set the bar high for what was expected of you as an employee and made sure you met those expectations—not being afraid to point out what you could have done differently if you didn't complete the task properly.

One attribute that Mrs. Shulman always embodied, which I truly admired, was being open to suggestions in improving the system or process of their retail operations, whether it was regarding the warehouse or the retail portion of the store.

Both Bernie and Terry Shulman were at the store from opening to closing, seven days a week—always setting an example for others to follow. My relationship with Bernie was short, as he passed away just one year after I started at Shulman's. When I think back now, part of me believes Bernie was mentoring or preparing me for something more than just working in the warehouse at the time.

Terry Shulman was my first mentor in the business world until I went on my own in the mid-80s. She allowed me to not only grow as a person but empowered and prepared me to be an entrepreneur as I pursued other retail and business ventures.

To this day, 40+ years later, I still think of them both as a part of my introduction to the world of business. No education in the world would have taught me the principles and real-time experiences I learned while at Shulman's.

Sometimes you don't realize how much someone has impacted you while working and spending time with them until their passing—then it's too late to tell them how you really feel and how much you appreciated them in your life.

So, in the case of Bernie and Terry Shulman, even though they are not here today, I want the both of them and their family to know how much I appreciated everything they did for me. They truly helped to make me the entrepreneur, business owner, mentor and coach I am today.

If you have someone who has touched or mentored you in yourlife, regardless if it's a teacher, friend, family member, co-worker or someone else you've associated with on a professional or personal level, make sure you let them know how much you appreciate them being part of your life.

Don't wait until it's too late to tell them how much they impacted you and made a difference in your life.

3 RISKING IT ALL TO SUCCEED

*"Even though I live
every day believing
that failure is not an
option, I embrace my
failures because they
take me one step
closer to success."*

-Larry Kemick

IT WAS SPRING 1993, and after several other business ventures and investments related to the retail industry—some positive and some not-so-positive—I was ready to seek out a new business opportunity and try something different.

As much as I loved, and basically grew up in the retail industry working with some of the most respected individuals in the country, it was time for a change. It created a significant part of what I didn't realize at the time would be the foundation for my future success, and for that, I was thankful. After much due diligence, my wife and

I decided to secure the rights to specific areas/markets related to the magazine publishing industry.

At the time, neither of us knew anything about publishing magazines. However, I knew marketing and advertising, and we both knew the importance of customer service and how to take care of people, so what the heck—it sounded like an awesome opportunity.

The idea, or should I say the interest, came from one of my previous sales reps in the drug store industry who formerly worked for Colgate Palmolive. He left his position to start the same type of magazine publishing business I was about to enter into.

After investigating the opportunity and looking at geographical areas still available throughout North America, we made the decision to move across the United States. We would ultimately open multiple markets over the next seven years in Oregon and Washington.

For most couples, this would have been an easy move and an incredible opportunity, right? What I'm not telling you is that we lived in Sarasota, Florida at the time, which was well over three thousand miles away. We didn't know a single soul on the entire west coast. I also had children whom we shared custody of every other week at each other's homes; this would now make things extremely emotional and trying for everyone, due to the geographical distance involved.

Unfortunately, my latest investment in the retail industry had placed us in a challenging financial position, so we weren't in any position to get ourselves involved in another business venture that wouldn't be assuredly successful. Our next move had to be the right move going forward; learning from all mistakes made prior.

After spending months researching and traveling to over a half-dozen markets across the United States, my wife and I finalized the area we were going to relocate to for the launch of our first magazine title. We were excited about this new opportunity.

After executing our agreement with the parent company representing the titles we just secured, we were thrilled to meet with my in-laws to share about our new business opportunity. We set up a time during the following weekend at one of our favorite restaurants near our home. As we walked into the restaurant, we made sure we had a large enough table in order to show them all the information we had compiled over the last six months.

We began to lay out our plans, sharing what we had just entered into, how excited we were and why we had chosen the area in which to relocate when my father-in-law interrupted me in mid-sentence. Without even letting us finish explaining our plans, our timeframe for the move, or what our business was even about; he began to express his disappointment loudly. To paint you a picture, this was the kind of "loud expressing" that makes everyone in the restaurant turn around to see what is happening—including language that you don't expect to hear in a family establishment.

He went on to tell us, point blank, that we were going to fail and be back in Florida within a year. Wow! What a blow.

As my wife and I both looked at each other in shock, it took everything in me to not say anything—I had never even heard my father-in-law raise his voice before. However, now was not the time to continue any discussions. I slowly got up from the table, took my wife's hand, and we quietly left the restaurant.

As we walked to the car and got in, neither of us said a word. I think we were both too stunned. We sat there in the parking lot in disbelief. I am not sure what I expected, but we both came to the conclusion that we were now on our own.

That was one of the most painful experiences we had encountered early on as a married couple, but it made us realize we had a bigger dream than anyone could understand at the time. We hoped that with some time and patience, they would come around at some point. Later on, as she looked back at what had taken place; my mother-in-law would say that she was mortified by what had happened and what her husband had said.

At the time, no one was totally aware of the true financial situation we were strapped with. As a matter of fact, my father-in-law wasn't the only one who gave us less than a year before we would be moving back to Florida.

After driving both of our vehicles over 3,100 miles to the new area we were about to call home, and using every dime of our remaining savings to launch our new business venture, the real eye-opener was when the 40' moving truck arrived in Oregon with all our personal possessions. There was no turning back after that—we had to make our new business venture a success, or I would be seeking other employment to pay rent and put food on the table.

Ultimately, our experience in representing specific magazine titles under the publishing company we contracted with lasted ten amazing years, with overwhelming success.

I'll never forget one of the first company regional meetings my wife, and I attended in the mid-90s when I had the opportunity to finally talk and meet with the executive team members who were representing the magazine titles we had just launched.

After the meeting, I asked about acquiring the rights to a variety of additional areas/markets and titles that were not part of my original plan or agreement with the company at that time.

They all looked at me and sarcastically responded: "Brad is a publisher with the company less than two years, and he wants to accomplish the world by expanding into all these other markets."

Maybe I just had a bigger vision than most others had seen or taken advantage of with the company, and now it was time to make that vision happen moving forward.

During our time with the publishing company we represented, my wife and I developed incredible relationships, not just with fellow publishers, but with the executive team of the company. One person, in particular, stood out to us—Barry Cohen, who was the VP of operations of the magazine titles we represented.

My wife and I considered Barry to be not just a mentor and friend, but someone we looked up to as he clearly lived by the twelve intangibles as outlined in Chapter One.

> "I have had the privilege of serving over 300 successful independent entrepreneurs over the years in the Publishing and the Residential Appliance industries. Brad and Cathy Taylor's insightful systems, ethical practices and magical ability to mentor people into industry-leading business owners, sets the standards for all of us to follow."
>
> *-Barry Cohen*

Throughout our term with the company, we opened 17 titles and received dozens of awards, becoming one of the largest, if not the largest publisher throughout their network of over 400+ magazine publications and titles. We accomplished what no other publisher with the company at the time had ever done; both in markets opened, number of pages printed collectively and in the selling of the magazine titles we owned.

Between 2000-2005, we sold all our interest in the magazine titles we represented, started our own multi-media marketing and publishing business and relocated from Oregon to Northern California.

Writing this book has allowed me to share the life lessons we encountered and learned throughout our journey. The struggles, challenges, and adversities we faced along the way made us stronger in both business and working together as a married couple—all while balancing children, family, and business.

I would say, without a doubt, that taking the risk to move across the country and going against the advice of many turned out to be a great success for us.

If you can take one thing from this book and utilize it personally—either in the company you work for, in your own company or in future business ventures moving forward—it was worth the time spent in sharing our journey with you. I hope you are challenged to take a risk in order to see your biggest dreams realized.

> "When I'm 80 years old and sitting with you on the front porch, I would rather be saying, 'I can't believe we did it,' than 'I wish we had done it."
>
> -Larry Kemick

4 PERSISTENCE IN SALES

"Being persistent is to be able to consistently function despite extremely difficult opposition, obstacles and disappointments along the way."

THIS CHAPTER IS a huge part of the success and journey of learning, understanding and mastering the art of sales, as well as navigating rejection. Even the pain of rejection has never stopped the pursuit of whatever goal my wife and I set out to accomplish.

As I mentioned in Chapter One, if I had to pick just one word that truly defined being successful in business, it would be PERSISTENCE—without question.

When my wife and I decided to move to Oregon to start up our advertising and publishing business, not only did we not completely understand the advertising/publishing industry at the time, but we also knew very little about sales and the proper methods of prospecting clients. What I did know was how to build a start-up, and how important customer service and customer relationships were in operating a successful, sustainable business model.

In the retail industry, I was on the other side of the desk, with everyone selling me everything from literal soup to nuts—not to mention pitching me all types of promotional/branding materials, print, radio and billboard advertising.

As I look back today, knowing the challenges sales reps are confronted with day in and day out, I probably should have been a little nicer to some of the reps trying to earn my business.

I guess, for me, it wasn't in my DNA to give up, especially at the time of the move. I had no choice but to succeed—there was no turning back. We had just moved across the United States, and my father-in-law gave us less than a year before we would be back. Those words both haunted and significantly motivated me to succeed over the next several years.

"Never mistake activity for achievement."
-John Wooden

My personal interpretation of persistence may be different than that of others, especially in building a sustainable brand and business. Here are two examples outlining what I have both witnessed and experienced over the years in business.

1. When a person gives up everything to accomplish a goal, regardless of whether it is personal or business-related, they will be persistent, tenacious and have a burning desire to succeed. This persistence is shown regardless of the obstacles, challenges, struggles, sacrifices, and disappointments along the way.

2. When someone sets a goal for themselves, yet they have already defined a backup plan in case their goal is not achieved, they will more than likely fail to ever achieve their set goal. This person was never 110% committed, so persistence now became work and it was easier to move to their backup plan so they wouldn't have to sacrifice, struggle, and endure any disappointment. This would be a very different story if they continued being persistent and consistent in achieving the goals they originally set out to accomplish.

> **When you have a backup plan, you've admitted you're not confident you will succeed."**

PERSISTENCE

PATIENCE

ENTHUSIASM

RESILIENCE

STRENGTH

INTENTIONAL

SELFLESSNESS

TENACITY

ENGAGE

NONNEGATIVE

CONSISTENCY

EFFORT

*"**PERSISTENCE** CREATES*
***CREDIBILITY** OVER TIME."*

I have personally witnessed entrepreneurs start up a business, only to see that business not even make it a year. This is because the entrepreneur did not have the persistence, confidence, and burning desire to succeed at any cost. If they had just exercised persistence instead of taking the easy road out, they would be extremely successful today.

To me, persistence is staying focused and just doing the work, day after day. It is staying the course and NEVER second-guessing the decision and goals you set.

My team always knew never to come to me with: "I don't think we can do that," because I would always respond with the same answer: "Let's figure out a way to make it happen."

There is always a solution to a problem, and it's usually right in front of you. But we are usually too focused on the problem to see that the solution is in plain sight.

> **Persistence is the path to success.
> Consistency is the vehicle you arrive in."**

INTENTIONAL SUCCESS IN SALES

Being persistent in sales isn't a bad thing if executed properly and professionally. When I started selling advertising in the mid-90s, the internet was just becoming a part of everyday business and life. We weren't using email as frequently as we do presently, nor were we using PDFs, Dropbox, social media or texting. We definitely didn't have a website to promote or utilize for selling purposes like we do today. In those days, we picked up the phone, set up an appointment and went to their office giving presentations face-to-face, all while developing true relationships along the way.

When I first started in sales, my selling tools were a pager, a bag phone (aka a cellphone) which cost a fortune per minute to talk on, and a landline with an answering machine.

Today, there is every type of technology out there to grow your business while prospecting, selling, marketing, and branding the product or services you represent. But, for some reason, it seems that individuals today are always looking for instant gratification—especially in sales. They are looking for the easy way to interact, thinking that technology will replace the high-touch approach to building true relationships. As the saying goes:

> "An email will never replace a handshake or face-to-face interactions."

Don't get me wrong; I love technology and social media. They are incredible selling tools in lead generation, branding, and marketing the products and services you represent while driving traffic to your website—if structured and executed properly. But, at the end of the day, it's the high-touch interactions with your clients that truly create and build long-term, lasting relationships structured on a foundation of credibility, transparency, and trust.

CREATING UNIQUE VALUE

Over the years, when my wife and I operate magazine titles ourselves, publishers and entrepreneurs throughout the country would ask us how we were able to keep our growth and revenue consistent in the magazine titles we personally operated.

First, I utilized the twelve intangibles of success. Additionally, I was hungry to succeed, focused on the task at hand, practiced persistence, and created unique value. I hustled to sell every page in every magazine we personally operated, understanding that "no" is not always "no." I was always thinking outside the box (being creative) for ways to drive potential clients to look at what we represented—without ever devaluing the brand by lowering the price point.

It would drive me crazy when potential clients I was prospecting or presenting to would share with me what our competitors were doing in discounting their pricing. This would always lead to them asking if I would be doing the same, and my response would always be the same—NO.

Regardless if you are in sales, retail, hospitality or the service industry, you need to become a master of "creating unique value" in the brand, product or services you are representing. This will assist you in differentiating yourself from others in your industry.

Again, this is something most people struggle with. It's hard to get your price if you know deep down you haven't truly created any value and don't have the belief and confidence in what you are currently doing.

For my wife and I, a portion of our success was being the very best in creating value—always striving to be a solution provider, consultant, and influence in the brand and services we represented.

This was defined in the following measures: product placement, customer service, regularly communicating with our clients and truly listening to them, the positioning of their brand, having the best story about the brand and selling that story, testimonials, and online digital/social exposure.

My goal was to consistently add something of unique value to our business every month, month after month.

One day, I was meeting a predominant realtor representing a high-end national real estate company. They told me that they didn't discount their commission like some of their colleagues did. They shared their presentation portfolio with me, where they outlined all the expenses they incur when taking on a listing. All their expenses were outlined in detail from start to finish.

Why did they do this? They were creating and capturing unique value in all the services they performed. They shared everything they did to represent and sell a listing, differentiating themselves from others who chose to do the minimum (and were forced to discount their commissions).

My wife and I didn't have a lot of turnover in the clientele we represented over the years because we were always skillfully communicating with our clients every chance we could. We were constantly educating them on everything we were bringing to the table to create unique value in helping them grow their business, generate leads, differentiate themselves from others and market the brand they worked so hard to represent.

We also didn't rely on just talking with them over the phone or text (a big mistake a lot of people in sales do today), especially as technology and the paradigm of web, digital, and social media has transformed. It was important to us to meet with our clients in person—face-to-face—whenever possible. Regardless of how long they were clients of ours, or how far they were from our office, we vowed to never take them for granted.

> **Our mission was to do what no one else wanted to take the time to do in order to grow their business."**

As I look back at the thousands of clients I have prospected over the years, I've found that researching the company and/or person you are going to contact is incredibly important in understanding their "WHY" in becoming a client. This process is also structured in understanding how their company makes purchasing decisions, so your actions are based on the interest, need, clarity, impact, vision, execution, and desire for what you are presenting. When my wife and I personally ran magazines years ago, we utilized the action of deadlines to facilitate decisions being made short and long-term.

> **Adults are like kids in many ways—they will test you before they trust and respect you."**

THE ART OF FOLLOWING UP

Before there were social networks and emails to introduce, market or brand yourself, I was picking up the phone and introducing myself in person, in group settings or at networking events.

This allowed me to put the brand I was representing behind the face that was calling to set up an appointment, as our brand was a direct reflection of who we were and the business we represented.

The biggest problem in sales today is that if you don't get the person on the phone at the time of making the call, most individuals won't follow up if they don't have a returned call after a voicemail is left. Maybe part of that is the fear of rejection, or maybe it is just lazy or complacent.

Today, more than ever before, people are busy with life in general. Maybe they had a hectic week, a bad day (or month), have been on vacation or are going through personal struggles.

If you aren't following up on a regular basis with potential clients (prospects), why are you even in sales? Furthermore, it's not just in sales that you need persistence—it also applies to all aspects of running your business, organization and your personal life as well.

PERSISTENCE PAYS OFF

I will never forget the story a friend of mine—who was a doctor and owned his own medical practice—shared with me years ago. He told me that once a week, at a set time, he would allow pharmaceutical and other sales reps to come into his medical practice and pitch and promote the products or services they were representing.

He would make it clear that the reps would need to come back multiple times before he would allow their products or services to be represented, utilized and promoted in his practice.

Why did he do this? For one thing, to ensure that they were not there for a quick sale. He wanted to make sure they really wanted to earn his business, and that they were there to service his practice long-term while also looking out for his best interests. He was amazed by how many professionals representing major companies pitched to him and never came back or followed up.

Remember, there are hundreds of thousands of products and services being pitched at any given time. You have one chance to make that contact and presentation count.

I believe it starts with your posture—how are you presenting yourself and how are you dressed. When meeting someone for the first time, are you shaking their hand firmly, creating eye contact? But most importantly, are you being relatable by listening to them talk instead of dominating the conversation?

In the media industry I came from, it would be nothing to make multiple calls—heck, sometimes I would be making dozens of calls before getting a specific prospect on the phone.

My rule was that if I were targeting a qualified lead (by doing my homework and researching,) I would call them a minimum of once a quarter until they became a client. I made it a point to never give up on them; always professionally following up. I could name hundreds of prospects that took months of following up—sometimes even years—before they became clients.

Ultimately, it was the persistence and consistency that truly created credibility for what I was representing and the true value I was creating for their business.

What's interesting is, most of those prospects who turned into clients turned out to be some of the best relationships we ever developed over the years.

PROSPECTING AND SHARING YOUR STORY

Here is where sales reps make a big mistake—they finally get their prospect on the phone and talk way, way too much. They never let the person they are calling get two words in, which ultimately ends the call in the words, "I'm not interested."

When you are prospecting someone, especially for the first time, the conversation needs to be short. Your goal is to set up a meeting in person—not to give them a full presentation over the phone. I dedicate hours and hours to training and reviewing this exact thing. It's not about us; it's about creating the "WHY" they would be interested in wanting to meet with you. After all, it's your job to know and understand your purpose in selling before you sell anything to someone else.

> **If your customers know you have a sincere vested interest in their success, they will become customers for life."**

If you are just trying to sell all the features and benefits of your product or services over the phone, why should they ever meet with you in person? You have just told them everything, including the pricing—that is, if they haven't already tuned you out and hung up.

With that said, if your sales pitch is strictly based on the features and benefits and do not include stories as part of your presentation, the brand you are representing is less likely to stand out from other products or services that may be competitive in your market.

It is the stories that people will remember; stories are what create an emotional connection to what you are representing. People will remember a story over any written words, numbers, stats, or PowerPoint presentations.

"The key to sharing a story is to make the story believable and relatable, NOT just make something up. It's re-enacting something that has recently happened while creating credibility, so people will place trust in what you are sharing in your story."

Stories carry huge emotional weight. They are relatable and relevant and can place the person, group or audience you are sharing the story with in the proper mindset—allowing you to make your point eloquently.

In prospecting over the phone, I would say if you are on a call more than three minutes, you're talking way, way too much. Sometimes you just need to ask a question and STOP talking— something most people can't do because they are either too excited, too nervous or think they know everything and haven't developed proper phone etiquette yet.

TURNING A NO INTO A YES

Let's look at another common mistake made in sales. After it took multiple times to get an individual on the phone, the prospect says they are not interested in meeting with you at the current time. If you allow them to hang up and never ask the magic words, "Do you mind if I follow up with you?"—you have missed an opportunity to re-connect at a future date.

> **"We** don't call to sell. We call
> to set up an appointment."
>
> *-Tomas Martinez III*

This also applies when you finally land an appointment to do a presentation in person, regardless if it was with one individual or a group. Let's say the meeting went great and you are leaving in high spirits, but you never asked "for the sale," or worse yet, you never asked for a follow-up meeting.

Because either way, you blew it.

Think about how long it took to get that appointment. Now you will spend countless days, weeks and months chasing down something you could have left with.

I have personally witnessed sales reps turning off potential clients they were trying to connect with or prospect by leaving irritating voicemails, texting the person to ask why they haven't returned their voicemail or sending multiple emails to ask why they aren't returning their calls.

When it comes to sales today, especially when sending an email:

1. The subject title needs to be short, simple, clear, specific and to the point.

2. You need to create unique value in your email while having a "call-to-action" statement with NO MORE than three paragraphs containing no more than two lines per paragraph. Anything more than that, and you have basically wasted your time and theirs. They will likely view your email first on their mobile device and then delete it if there is no reason to save.

I can't tell you how many times I've heard the word NO, which ultimately turned into a YES. But, at the end of the day, it is persistence and patience that are professionally executed which will create credibility—and credibility always leads the way.

CONSISTENCY

Being consistent is working to accomplish your ultimate goals. Consistency is like running a marathon—not a sprint. A marathon is a long-term race, but a sprint is a short-term goal with a set time to finish. There is a difference between persistence and consistency but combined they will give you the results you worked so hard to accomplish.

Hearing rejection over and over is hard, especially when you're not getting the results you want.

In business, sales or even in your personal life, being consistent is hugely important in achieving not just activity, but measurable results. Most people will switch to something else if they don't see immediate results in what they are striving to accomplish. Being consistent in executing your plan is critical for long-term sustainability.

THE IMPORTANCE OF SYSTEMS

Several years ago, when my wife and I sold a publication that was incredibly successful, I attached as part of the sale agreement an exhibit which I called "The Blueprint in Maintaining a Strong, Sustainable Magazine." This was from ten years' experience in the market that specific magazine title was operated in. This was basically the "system" that would allow the buyer to continue the process of growing the magazine we turned over. This would also let the buyer know that if the system and processes outlined in the exhibit were not followed, the buyer could jeopardize the current overall success.

It was not our intention to deter the buyer from bringing new ideas, creativity, services, and passion to the magazine. We just wanted to make sure that the buyer understood that the outlined system—which allowed the magazine title to prosper over many years—was proven and consistent in providing enormous value to the clients who had routinely been advertising in the magazine since day one.

> For my wife and I, it has always been about
> the clients and the value we consistently
> created to help grow their business."

This is where franchises struggle in the business world, some-times due to the franchisee not understanding that there is a system for a reason—and that not completely following the system will significantly impact their ability to succeed. There is a saying in running a business or franchise that goes:

> Not following 100% of a system
> is like not breathing air."

I have seen individuals leave training from major companies and say to themselves, "I can do it a better way."

Then the months go by, and that person is struggling because they are trying to "reinvent the wheel" instead of following the blueprint of success that was already laid out for them by the company they are representing or just invested in.

In my industry, the people who consistently follow the system are exceptionally successful. The ones who don't will struggle and ultimately fail; not necessarily due to their lack of effort, money or background, but because they are trying to reinvent the wheel of proven success.

CONSISTENCY IS KEY

I'm constantly sharing about the importance of consistency and patience through the example of cultivating and preparing the soil for planting seeds. After you have prepared the soil, you will need to fertilize the seeds and water them. Finally, you will watch the seeds you planted slowly start to germinate, grow and come into existence.

Let's explore how the idea of consistency plays out in the following two examples:

1. **Starting up social media sites.**

    Business owners and professionals of all industries will go to a social media seminar or conference where there are professional speakers with years of experience talking about all the benefits of properly setting up business social media sites.

    There they will learn how to gain customer insights, increase brand awareness, lead generation, metrics, increase web traffic, post content, build trust and brand awareness with the audiences they are targeting. Exciting, right?

They leave the seminar all fired up, excited about launching multiple social media sites with the intention of implementing exactly what they have just been taught.

The first several months go by, and everything is looking great. Then, after six months, the social media sites start to have less and less content, followers, and shared posts, until they are basically abandoned.

What happened? There was not a commitment to being consistent. This played out in the inconsistent execution of the plan to launch the social media sites, which ultimately made their business and the brand they are representing look very unprofessional. This same scenario can go for...

2. **Joining a gym.**

It's the first of the year, and you want to lose weight or simply get in better shape. You get a gym membership and start going every day, which then slides to every other day. Eventually, you are only going once a week, which ultimately ends up with you not going at all.

Why? Again, the commitment wasn't truly there.

That's why consistency is hugely important—not just in business, but in your personal and family life as well.

Remember: it's the persistence and consistency that will create credibility and authenticity in growing the brand, product, and services you represent.

BEING SUCCESSFUL

IS JUST DOING THE WORK.

PERSISTENCE

+

CONSISTENCY

=

ACTIVITY

&

RESULTS

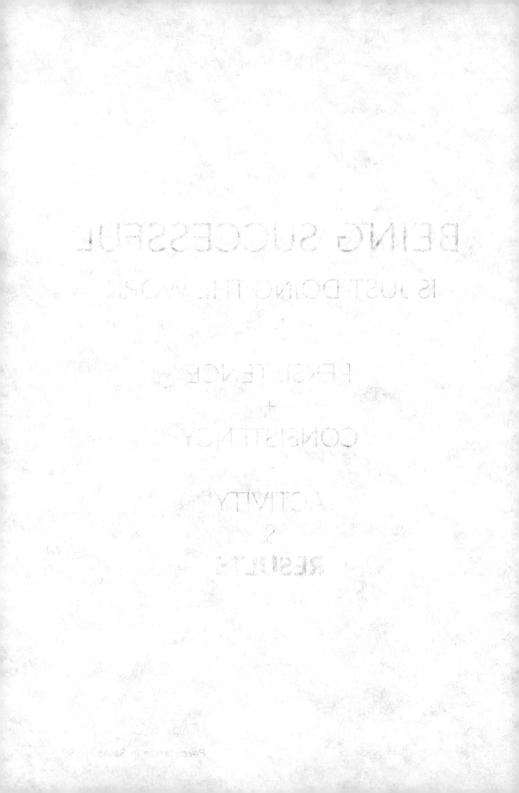

5 TIME MANAGEMENT & GOAL SETTING

"Anything you truly measure will improve over time."

STAYING ORGANIZED

BEING ORGANIZED AND having great time management skills is a huge part of the habits you create daily in order to take your career and business to the next level. It can make the difference between being reactive and proactive in running your company.

I remember purchasing my first Franklin Planner in the mid-80s. I loved going to the Franklin store at the mall to see what new accessories they displayed to keep me organized and on task. It's only been in the last five years that I have transitioned my planner to a tablet—syncing my calendar, contacts, and tasks with my laptop, cloud and mobile devices.

With that said, I still utilize a journal every day, writing down my thoughts, ideas, notes, conversations, and goals.

I would suggest that everyone, regardless of what you do in life—even if you're retired or a stay-at-home parent—keep a daily log of thoughts, ideas, notes and tasks to perform in a journal.

You will find yourself going back countless times to seek out the priceless information you had previously written down. This is much more efficient than looking for that floating piece of paper, legal pad, back of an envelope or sticky note you placed somewhere... that you may now never recover because it's probably been thrown out or misplaced.

> **The best-kept secret of the rich is not genius or brilliance, it's the management of time."**
>
> *-Jim Rohn*

When our kids were smaller, my wife and I heard a speaker talk about planning your week out together as a couple every Sunday. We applied that principle not just as the kids were going through school, sports, and events we needed to attend, but throughout our lives. To this day, we still regularly review our schedules together as a couple.

Utilizing this process together over the years reduced the unknowns and stress in day-to-day family activities we would have potentially missed if we weren't organized and in sync with everything happening around us.

I'm a big believer in organization. I see professionals today struggle with a lack of organization and time management, which unfortunately reflects in their daily performance in both their personal and professional life.

One day, one of my older children told me a saying they heard in one of their classes at college years ago: "If you're early, you're on time. If you're on time, you're late. If you're late, why are you even showing up?"

We've probably all heard this saying before (potentially in different words), but at the end of the day, it truly speaks volumes. Your actions in life—including organization and time management—are a direct reflection of who you are as a person.

Regardless of what you do, putting the proper time management skills in place will help with procrastination, keep you focused and on task, allow you to brainstorm, bring clarity to what you want to achieve, allow you to leverage your time wisely and help you create written timelines and execute them. This will allow you to prioritize your schedule to have less stress in the daily, weekly and monthly activities you have on your calendar.

GOAL-SETTING STRATEGIES

Setting goals, and the execution of these goals involves much more than just writing something down on a piece of paper or verbally expressing your intentions without a set plan in place.

By understanding your purpose and your why, you gain a sense of direction, vision, meaning, clarity, feeling of accomplishment and true fulfillment when the goal is completed.

Here are ten strategic principles that will allow you to tackle any goal you set for yourself.

1. **Knowledge**

   First and foremost, you must be incredibly knowledgeable on the specific goal you have identified—well before the execution of the goal. Do your homework, research, and become the expert. Remember: your greatest competitive advantage is knowledge.

2. **Purpose**

   Be crystal clear in creating your action plan and write it down. Establish your why and your purpose, and make sure you are comfortable and confident in being able to sell them to others—both within your organization and outside your organization.

3. **Attitude**

   Your attitude, passion, enthusiasm, posture, and relatability will be instrumental in executing your plan. Be mindful that there will be a learning curve throughout the process and give yourself the grace to learn.

4. **Commitment**

   Make a commitment and stick to it. Remember to continue challenging yourself and your team to stretch out of their comfort zones to accomplish the set objective—regardless of whether it is a short or long-term goal.

5. **Details**

Remember, it's all about the details, so dot your I's and cross your T's. Be thorough, be creative, and think outside the box.

6. **Timeline**

Come up with a timeline/schedule outlining—in detail—what you want to accomplish. Use a step-by-step process, breaking the goal into smaller tasks (baby steps if necessary). Make sure you are being realistic in creating a completion date, as this will give you and your team more clarity, direction, vision, and confidence.

Remember, measurable goals play out over time. They should be intentionally thought through—not spontaneous—allowing you to create changes in your thought process.

7. **Challenges**

Be prepared for setbacks, objections, and adversities along the way. Learn from your mistakes and don't allow distractions and negativity to interfere with the process.

8. **Progress**

Monitor and track your progress and actions. Review the progress multiple times a week to stay on-track until completed. Stay focused—it's okay to be a little obsessive! Be persistent and consistent and reflect on your why and purpose throughout the journey toward accomplishing your goal.

9. **Collaborate**

   Get feedback from others. They will bring knowledge, insight, suggestions, and collaboration throughout the process. Be aware of your weaknesses—it's okay to outsource specific tasks to professionals in and outside your field. But remember who's in charge—it's your credibility on the line.

10. **Celebrate**

    Regardless if your goal is small or large, celebrate and let others know how much you appreciated their hard work in helping you (and your team) accomplish your goals.

> "When you focus on the small and
> simple things in life and business,
> it prepares you to accomplish the
> large and great things over time."
>
> *– Emile Bonfiglio*

VISUAL GOAL SETTING

> "Visualization is one of the most
> powerful mind exercises you can do."

For my wife and I, goal setting is an instrumental part of achieving big goals.

I'm a big believer in visual goal setting—even today, with all the technology and apps available. I learned this over the years early on in growing our publishing businesses.

When we moved to Oregon in the early '90s, we rented a home for the first two years before securing our first office to work out of. I transformed the entire dining/living room into our office. There wasn't an empty space on the walls that didn't represent someone, something or a company I was targeting as a potential client.

Basically, I ripped out ads, articles from magazines, mailers, flyers and newspapers (you must remember, the internet in the early '90s wasn't what it is today to do research). If they were in my area, related to my industry and qualified as a potential client to target, they were on my walls, and I was going after them. I would wake up every morning and visualize future clients/prospects hanging on my walls. They would stay up until they became a client and let me tell you: seeing them constantly was motivation in itself. Not to mention it irritated the heck out of me every day that they weren't yet my clients.

Some would argue that with all the technology out there today, you could accomplish the same thing with a well-organized excel spreadsheet or a CRM (customer relationship management) system.

My response is: yes, you could. However, a spreadsheet is not a CRM, and in sales today, having a good CRM is priceless. It allows you to retain all the history, analytics and communications with your clients and prospects.

A good CRM—in addition to an old-fashioned vision board—will help facilitate achieving specific tasks or goals you have set.

In 1994, our first magazine title grew from 16 to 180 pages over several years by using visual goal setting. As I expanded into other areas, I encouraged my team to implement visuals to stay focused and accomplish their goals.

Visuals put your PLAN into action."

Even in our office today, 25+ years later, we measure specific tasks on a 5' x 8' whiteboard outlined by month. These tasks are also duplicated on an internal cloud-based system.

You see, as much as technology has advanced over the years, placing the same information on a spreadsheet, CRM or web-based platform will not have the same motivation as a visual that you look at on a daily basis.

Today, vision boards can be utilized in a variety of applications in both business and personal daily life, including wedding planning, goal setting, family organization, and dream building.

An article I read several years ago shared that creating a sacred space that displays what you want actually does bring it to life.

> What we focus on expands... When you create a vision board and place it in a space where you constantly are viewing it multiple times a day, you essentially end up doing short visualization exercises throughout the day."

Goals that are measured weekly, monthly and annually will improve over time, but, as the saying goes, "a goal without a timeline is just a dream."

Regardless of what goals you desire to achieve, being accountable to someone will help you accomplish them much faster than acting alone. With that said, the goals you are setting need to be realistic and they should stretch you to get out of your comfort zone in order to see them realized.

As I mentor individuals today in achieving their goals with their team, I like to share the analogy of leading by example.

Years ago, I would use my calendar as an example of what I was doing so others could see what allowed me to be successful in the industry I was in. I would teach the principles of setting up appointments, presentations, and events I would attend on a consistent basis. I made sure I was demonstrating the number of calls, appointments, and presentations I would have every week, month after month. I explained that part of goal setting is not missing opportunities—if you have openings in your calendar, those are considered missed opportunities.

Your calendar should be organized and reviewed regularly to make sure you are slating time throughout each day to be as efficient as you can, placing time slots for prospecting, communication, presentations, meetings, returning emails, etc.

When my wife and I were still running a magazine title, I would have a contest with another member of our team to see who would make the most calls a day, a week, or a month. A long time ago, I learned that you can never ask someone to do something you are not willing to do yourself. Leading by example is incredibly powerful in growing your brand and organization.

"If I wanted my team to be successful, I needed to lead by example, sharing what made us successful."

I remember going to an annual publishing conference in the mid-90s and meeting a publisher on the East Coast who had a magazine with a very high page count (in the hundreds of pages). When I came back from that conference, I brought back several copies of their magazine and set them on my desk, next to my sink at home.

I looked at it every day, saying to myself, "If they can do that, I can do that too!" It's all about VISUAL goal setting!

CRUNCHING NUMBERS AND WRITING BUSINESS PLANS

Finally, goal setting also needs to align with your business plan. It is simply not enough to be strategic in setting up goals and vision boards; you must know where you are financially in order to continue to grow.

Business owners need to know their numbers, sales and how to read a Profit and Loss Statement (P & L). If you don't know your numbers, it's hard, if not impossible, to grow a profitable business with achievable and measurable goals.

If you are a business owner, now is a great time to ask yourself the following questions: do you create a business plan for your company at the end of every year, updating your plan multiple times a year, reevaluating your goals, objectives, and numbers on a consistent basis?

If not, there is no time like the present to start!

6 STRUGGLES & LESSONS LEARNED

"Every successful entrepreneur has faced adversity; it's how you choose to move forward that will define your success."

WORK ETHIC

HAVING A GREAT work ethic is not just working hard and putting in the time—it starts with having the proper attitude and determination in what you are seeking to accomplish.

This is something I have tried to teach my own children over the years. Your actions in life are a direct reflection of who you are as a person. Having a great attitude is incredibly important in all aspects of your life.

I was taught this early on by my dad, who worked as a chemical engineer for Standard Oil for 40+ years.

> **You** may not necessarily always love what you are doing, but it's still important to always give 100% in everything you are doing."

As we've all heard before: attitude is everything. We are always facing challenges in both our personal and professional lives. What matters is how you intentionally choose to deal with them.

My wife and I have faced countless trials in business over the years—struggles that would have caused most entrepreneurs and business owners to give up or pursue other ventures. At the end of the day, the trials in life will play out according to how you choose to deal with them.

If you are not facing obstacles, challenges and struggles in your business, you are probably in "idle mode." This means you have become complacent in your day-to-day activities.

How you walk through trials is what will make you a better person, leader, and entrepreneur.

> **There** is no secret sauce for success... it's simply the result of doing the work, being authentic and having a great work ethic."

Recently, I had a conversation with a business owner who had an unfortunate experience with one of their major vendors. At first, the business owner was incredibly disappointed and frustrated with the response from their vendor after receiving several emails and having a phone conversation regarding the problem that had just transpired. They felt that the vendor was not looking out for their best interests and didn't care about the clients they represented.

When I talked with the business owner regarding the unfortunate experience, I suggested immediately setting up a time to meet in person with the vendor. This is a much better option than trying to communicate by email, text or phone with the person who was their immediate contact. I explained to the business owner that emails and texts can be misinterpreted, not to mention they can cause a delay in solving the problem. Meeting in person or setting up a conference call with all the parties involved would be the right thing to do at this point.

When there is a situation that needs immediate attention, I'm a big believer in either calling the person or meeting with them in person vs. email or text. You can't read the person's emotions when you go through email, but you can when you're having a real-time conversation.

The next day, the business owner set up a time to meet with the vendor and their team. Because they were located near the vendor, they could arrange to meet at their corporate office. I gave the business owner suggestions on how to approach the meeting and encouraged them not to go in with a negative attitude, regardless of what had just transpired. Remember: it's all about your attitude in dealing with the situation.

When I talked with the business owner after their meeting that afternoon, the attitude of the business owner was completely different. This was not because the situation was resolved, but because both parties came to the table with the willingness to figure out the problem—not pointing blame on any one person. They made the decision to stay until the situation was thoroughly looked at and resolved.

This was critical to figuring out what caused the problem initially and coming up with a solution to prevent the problem from reoccurring moving forward.

As you'll remember from previous chapters, relatability is all about listening. If you approach a problem with high emotion, always pointing the blame, not willing to listen to others and vocalizing a bad attitude, the situation will escalate to a potentially disastrous level.

You are now representing yourself, the brand and your company unprofessionally. Allowing a situation to get to this point is showing signs of weakness—particularly the unwillingness to properly assess the situation—or any future problems that may transpire moving forward.

The business owner told me they looked at this specific example with the vendor the same as they would look at a sales lead; making sure they were ending every communication with a follow-up time/date until everything was completely resolved.

With that said, I also explained to the business owner that it's okay to stand your ground as well. You can explain that the brand, product, and services you are representing are a direct reflection of the product or services you are receiving from the vendor. However, the vendor needs to clearly understand and know you are not willing to accept anything less in quality. You must do this professionally, yet firmly, in all your communications and interactions.

Remember, your posture is why people will take you seriously.

I have previously seen business owners refuse to accept any blame for a problem that could have been defused and resolved by simply listening to their customer rather than immediately becoming defensive.

I have learned over the years, and continue to share with professionals today, that with every problem there is an opportunity to learn and grow. These teachable moments are where you will not only learn from mistakes but hopefully prevent yourself from making the same mistake twice.

If I had to list every mistake I made over the last 40+ years, that could be a book in itself! The following lessons learned are just a few examples to avoid as an entrepreneur, executive or business owner, even if you are someone who is just thinking about starting their own business.

LESSON ONE | KNOW WHO YOU ARE HIRING

In the late '90s, we had an awesome publisher that represented several of our magazine titles. Unfortunately, they had to move back East due to a series of family issues that had transpired.

At the time, they had a graphic artist who also assisted with a variety of other responsibilities including customer service, sales, circulation, and design.

After a series of discussions with this individual, my wife and I decided that instead of looking for another publisher, we would hire the graphic artist as the new publisher. It only made sense to have someone who was already thoroughly familiar with their publication, clients, and the market they were represented in, take over the existing magazine titles. This was a win-win situation for everyone involved—not to mention an incredible opportunity for this person, right?

Well, here is the rest of the story: about six months after the new publisher took over the two magazine titles for us, we received an anonymous letter marked "confidential." It was from a long-term client representing a major company, letting us know that the new publisher was a "registered pedophile" and was on probation. Of course, they attached documentation confirming the letter we just received.

The letter stated the following:

> "To whom it may concern: the attached came across my desk. It is very disturbing to think I have been doing business with a person like this. In addition, this person is at clients' homes, etc. I and others have been delighted to do business with your company. Unfortunately, unless a change is immediately made, I will have no choice but to pull my advertising and I'm sure others will do the same as well."

What did we learn from this experience? Never—I repeat, NEVER—hire anyone without a complete background check, even if you may think you know the person you are hiring—something we were NOT doing at the time.

The takeaway from our learning lesson: have a complete background check done on anyone who represents your company. This is not limited to just employees but should include independent contractors who represent your business and your brand—regardless of how well or how long you have known the person.

LESSON TWO | PROTECTING YOUR BUSINESS

When we started our initial publishing business in the early '90s, we sacrificed everything to launch it; investing every dime we had left to our name.

For the first three years, we spent countless hours a day, seven days a week working without vacations. We lived in a rental home and basically lived our life around our business 24-7.

As we started to put together our team and rented our first office space, some individuals within our organization wanted instant gratification. They wanted to have what we had intentionally worked so hard and long to build; they saw what we were creating, but they weren't willing to put in the time, work or resources to have that success.

For me, there is nothing more gratifying and fulfilling than helping and mentoring someone to become tremendously successful.

Disappointment came in the early years when we didn't know any better. Some members of our team wanted the lifestyle we worked so hard to achieve but weren't willing to put in the effort that would allow them to reap the rewards of being successful. They weren't the ones who secured the rights, developed the relationships, put up the money, worked countless hours, and hustled with persistence and consistency. They were the ones who looked at other colleagues having success, expecting to have the same without doing the work.

Basically, they felt a sense of entitlement. Maybe part of this was because we were growing our business so rapidly. Within six years, we had opened over 14 magazine titles, becoming the largest publisher within the company we represented. When you have success in business, some people will go to great lengths to try to steal that success—regardless of how they get it.

We learned the hard way that you must protect your assets, accounts, databases, systems, and processes, etc. As much as you want to be able to trust everyone (that was me), unfortunately, life doesn't always work that way.

When we started our new media company in 2003, we sold the titles we had previously built up under the company we formerly represented. With the start of our new company, we required everyone to sign Non-Disclosure Agreements (NDAs) or Confidentiality Agreements, based on their position, to protect all our intellectual property moving forward. This included all vendors and independent contractors we partnered with for specific services rendered. We also worked with our attorneys to design agreements based on the position the person was being hired for, either in-house or representing one of our brands, thus preventing any misinterpretation of their responsibilities.

The most important thing I share with business owners today

regarding hiring is that people will tell you what you want to hear to get the job—regardless of the experience listed on their resume.

The real proof is watching their actions six months to a year later. Observe how they perform, how they communicate and interact with others—especially if they are a team player, looking out for the company's best interest.

LESSON THREE | CREATE A TEAM

Creating the right team and culture within your organization, regardless of how small or large your business is, is critical in setting up an infrastructure and foundation to be sustainable.

The saying "if you want it done right, do it yourself" will never allow you to grow your business and be sustainable.

As my wife and I built our team over the years, it was all about finding people with passion, integrity, great communication skills and the twelve intangibles reviewed in Chapter One. Of course, these individuals also embodied a willingness to be team players along the way.

To me, loyalty is everything, and something I place huge value on when running an organization.

When I get asked the magic questions, "What was the process of interviewing someone for your organization? What should I be looking for when hiring someone for my company today?"

I explain the formula that always worked for us...

"I'm not looking to date someone; I'm looking to get married to that person."

Here is the breakdown of what I mean in the above statement: our team would go through a vetting process when trying to find someone for a specific responsibility, position or area within our organization. I will say, our interview process is a bit different from other organizations.

As we would talk to people looking to be part of one of our brands, we would explain up front that our process takes a little longer than most. We are not looking to "date" you; we are looking to "get married" to you. This means that we are looking to build a long-term relationship that is beneficial for everyone involved.

I tell everyone that we are in a relationship-driven business, and those relationships start with the people who directly represent you, your brand and your culture, as well as the products and the services you offer. At the end of the day, that is what you and your company will be remembered for.

Finding incredible talent is the key, yet too many companies are too quick in bringing someone aboard without completely understanding the person they are looking to hire.

Not taking the time to have a series of conversations and interviews in order to truly understand their long-term intentions could cost you more time in damage control than you could ever imagine. My wife and I learned this the hard way over the years.

Taking the time to research the person you are looking to bring aboard is critical—checking their references, social media and most importantly, doing a complete background check.

When I'm personally involved in talking with someone for a specific position, I spend a lot of time speaking with them about what they would like to accomplish in both their personal and professional lives—i.e., what are their goals and dreams?

For many reasons, most people would never ask those questions. Maybe they just don't care, or they are trying to fill a position quickly. They also may be intimidated by the person they are interviewing and the qualifications they have outlined in their resume.

In my opinion, not asking those simple questions is a huge mistake.

Remember the story in a previous chapter when Bernie Shulman, the owner of the retail drug store, spent time to ask me personal questions about my life and future goals?

You see, you don't have to be hiring someone for an executive position to still be interested in what the person you are interviewing is looking to seek out in a career. You would be surprised at how your sincere interest in their success becomes an important part of the way they perceive you as an employer down the road.

As people seek out their next career path in life, they want to know that the company and the culture of the company they are looking to be part of cares about them. They want to be assured that their bosses are interested in their future and that they won't just become another number in the company's system.

In some scenarios, I like to meet with the potential candidate for lunch or dinner if possible, asking their significant other to join us. It's amazing what you will learn if you just take the time to listen with compassion and sincerity.

It is important to surround yourself with a team that is smarter than you—a team that will compliment you in your weaknesses and strengths. This is something that a lot of business owners and executives are uncomfortable with.

But, at the end of the day, it's your team that will make you successful. If you think for a moment, you can do everything on your own, you're only kidding yourself and placing a Band-Aid on your company's future growth—especially as technology and social media continue to evolve and positions are being dedicated to these areas.

LESSON FOUR | PROFESSIONAL ADVISERS

In addition to creating your team as outlined in lesson three, surrounding yourself with the proper professional advisers in accounting, legal and insurance is important in creating the proper infrastructure to operate a successful, profitable and sustainable business.

1. **Accounting Firm**

    It took us seven years—going through five CPAs—before we finally found an accounting firm that truly took the time to understand our business model. It was important to us to have someone who understood the way our company was structured and the way our agreements were written with our clients, due to the complexity of their term and payment schedule.

    A great accounting firm is built on experience, relationships, strategic planning, and support; looking out for the best interest of your company and being proactive in structuring future systems for long-term growth.

Unfortunately, this is something some smaller accounting firms and/or sole CPAs are not capable of doing on their own while representing businesses of multiple industries.

Your accounting firm also needs to collaborate with your legal team in understanding your business model to ensure that all the proper processes are in place to protect your business as it grows.

2. **Corporate/Business Law**

Finding the right law firm with expertise in corporate and business law is extremely important in protecting your company's interests and assets. This may include intellectual property, registered trademarks, patents, employee, independent contractor and client agreements, non-disclosure and confidential agreements, governmental issues, real estate law, and buy-sell agreements, just to name a few.

This affiliation is especially beneficial when you need legal advice or have contracts, agreements, or leases you would like reviewed before they are executed.

Your counsel understands your operations and will be looking out for you and your company's best interests.

3. **Litigation Law**

Years ago, when we faced our first litigation regarding our business, my wife and I were devastated by the approach and reason the lawsuit was filed—we had never been put in that position before. Unfortunately, if a lawsuit is filed against you or your company, your only "right" is to defend yourself. This costs a lot of money, and the outcome relies heavily on the strength of your legal team.

Our corporate attorneys referred us to a leading litigation firm that specialized in cases like ours.

Once we secured this firm—and even today as we sit down with them occasionally about specific issues—I'm a bit intimidated when I meet with them.

Once you have been taken advantage of, you learn your lesson and do everything you can to never let that situation happen to you or your business again. You take precautions by associating yourself with the best law firms that will always be protecting the businesses you worked so hard to build.

4. **Insurance**

Most business owners have multiple insurance providers based on specific needs in operating their companies and any real estate involved in those companies.

As I talk with entrepreneurs today who are operating a variety of businesses, retail, construction, restaurant, medical and franchise services, it's amazing how many of them do not have the proper business insurance needed to protect their company.

The one thing my wife and I have always done is have an annual meeting/review with all our insurance providers since the laws are constantly changing within the insurance industry. It's important to find insurance providers that are looking out for the best interest of your business, but it's still your responsibility to ask the right questions and challenge them if necessary.

If you are a business owner—regardless of the size of your organization, if you work from home or have an office, retail or service location—when was the last time you had a meeting to review ALL your business policies in detail with your providers?

When was the last time you took a complete inventory of all your business assets?

When was the last time you reviewed your employees' files and confirmed they have a current driver's license and insurance if they are driving your vehicles? You should have a rider on your business policy to cover them while they are driving for your business, even if it is just to the post office on their way home from work. This kind of rider is inexpensive and protects you and your business should anything happen to your employee while they are driving for anything related to your business.

When was the last time you reviewed your real estate property policies?

If you are a small business owner, do you have a personal umbrella policy?

These are just a few thoughts to review in order to protect you from heartache down the road if your policies are not properly structured and written.

LESSON FIVE | BACKING UP YOUR FILES

I remember it as if it were yesterday: it was 2001, and we were halfway through designing one of our magazine titles when the power went out in our office. We lost most of the files our designer spent days working on earlier that week.

After that disaster, we learned from our mistakes and bought both battery back-up and an external hard drive.

Today, with real-time cloud backup, syncing files, shared files, and automated security encryption, it makes life a lot easier knowing your files are safe and automatically backed—up. With that said—if you are not using a cloud-based or server backup platform—are you at least backing up your files to multiple external hard drives, keeping one off the premises for security purposes?

Another suggestion from our legal and accounting partners was to scan all the files from previous years, so you have both a digital and paper copy of anything of significance. Always make sure you are complying with privacy laws when collecting and storing customer information, including credit card numbers, addresses, etc.

LESSON SIX | PROFITABILITY OF YOUR BUSINESS

It took us several years—and multiple changes in professionals—to get our accounting and legal dialed into a team who would not only look out for our best interests but had the experience and wherewithal to help us manage a business as our growth scaled so we could be financially successful.

Just because someone is an accountant or an attorney does not mean that they have the proper knowledge and experience to manage higher revenue—even if they were recommended by someone you trust.

I will never forget sitting down with the second accountant we switched to after starting our business. On a side note, we learned that the first accountant's typical client earned less than 50k/year. Anyway, this second accountant was the first to tell us we had to know our numbers: sales, overhead, cost of goods sold, payroll, taxes, etc.

When he looked at our business reports, he wanted to know where all the money was. It was apparent to him that we had a decent amount of sales, but upon further review, we were not managing what we had well—or charging enough for our services.

He helped us to fine-tune our QuickBooks chart of accounts so that when we generated reports, we could clearly see how we were doing financially. We had to know the proper costs of goods related to the services we were providing, our profit margins and fixed expenses incurred in order to run our business.

LESSON SEVEN | WHY HAVE A BOOKKEEPER?

Why would you want to hire a bookkeeper when you are probably perfectly capable of doing it yourself—or so you think? Maybe you are still in the early stages of your business or perhaps it's because you want all the control!

Many small business owners think they are the best person to manage their business finances and bookkeeping. But you must decide where your time is best spent and focus on doing that which makes the best business sense—which will likely bring about the most profit for your business.

Finances and revenue are the heartbeat of your business. Without properly managed revenue, you will be out of business.

Again, this is part of creating a team of professionals that are going to help you manage and propel your business to the highest level of success possible.

As a small business owner, you should be 100% involved in and know/understand what is going on in your business. However, having a trained and knowledgeable bookkeeper will free you up to do those things you do best. Depending on the size of your business, you may need a bookkeeper as little as 4-6 hours a week to start.

One thing to consider, especially if you have direct relationships with your clients, is conflict of interest. This arises when you must solicit, sell and service a client and also call to collect money or chase them on past due accounts.

Conflict of interest can be very uncomfortable for both parties—not to mention having a bookkeeper will make your company appear more professional and will likely lead to a lower percentage of outstanding receivables.

Your bookkeeper will be working directly with your CPA/ accounting firm. Most bookkeepers are not accountants, which is why they don't come with the high hourly price tag of an accountant! If they are both working together, your bookkeeper can have everything organized, and in the formats the accountant needs— saving them time—and saving you money.

When hiring a bookkeeper, have them come to your office to work for you if possible, not remotely. This way they are working in a controlled environment, on your equipment—which does not leave your office.

Due to all the privacy laws, it is best to provide a dedicated office/computer that meets the requirements for storing contracts, data, QuickBooks, bank statements, checks, etc.

The other benefit is the ability to sit down with your book-keeper on a regular basis and review the reports and any spreadsheets you may have them consistently maintain.

Consult your local and state laws for the proper background checks you should run before hiring anyone in this position. Have a list of items that are important to you such as the following:

1. Accounting software proficiency
2. Document/spreadsheet proficiency
3. General accounting, payables and receivables experience
4. State level corporate filing knowledge
5. Communication and phone etiquette, as they will be speaking on your behalf with vendors and clients
6. Grammar, spelling and organizational skills
7. Transportation and DMV record

We hope that by sharing our own struggles and mistakes, you can take our lessons learned and apply them to your own business. Take inventory of your policies and procedures, do your homework before hiring someone, and make sure you have dedicated professionals to help you with your workload. Trust us, it will help you tremendously in the long run!

7 WORKING WITH YOUR SPOUSE

> *"The greatest marriages are built on teamwork. A mutual respect, a healthy dose of admiration and a never-ending portion of love and grace."*
>
> -Fawn Weaver

WORKING TOGETHER AS A COUPLE

WHEN MY WIFE and I moved to Oregon, I knew that she would play an important role in our company—I just didn't realize at the time how important a role it would be.

Initially, we didn't plan on working the business together full-time. My wife was a registered pediatric nurse, and she was happy to help with the day-to-day tasks needed to operate our business. She took charge of the bookkeeping and helped with a variety of administrative tasks while continuing to maintain her RN license part-time.

Within two years of launching our first magazine, we had also launched several other titles in adjacent markets. I was busy trying to keep my head above water; working seven days a week to juggle the responsibilities of maintaining and growing the business.

One day, I shared with my wife that our business really needed us to both be involved in the everyday operations instead of her working part-time as an RN. I suggested that we both invest full-time in growing our company as a couple. We decided that if we were going to be truly successful in the crazy business that we had we moved across the country to start up, it would take both of us working full-time to make that happen. We also knew that we had the same vision, dreams, and goals we ultimately wanted to achieve.

Within six months of making the decision to work together full-time, my wife phased out of the nursing profession she had worked so hard for. We have worked together ever since; never looking back or second-guessing the decision we made together.

"Moving to Oregon to start our business was a real leap of faith for Brad, and especially me.

We went out on the proverbial limb thinking, "this was going to work for us." We had no choice but to succeed intentionally, although the level of success was unknown and quite scary. It was 100% up to us. Failure would not be an option, period.

I had spent my life watching my dad and most everyone in my immediate family work hard and do well—but always as the employee of someone else's business.

When I decided to become a registered nurse, I was signing up for a life of the same: the familiar life of expecting the comfort of receiving a paycheck that was directly related to the hours I worked the previous week.

Marrying an entrepreneur was like learning a whole new language for me.

From the beginning, Brad was passionate about working hard and giving his all to his businesses.

It was very hard for me to comprehend how you could risk the consistency of a regular paycheck. We had a family to support; they depended on us. I always knew I could work more hours as a nurse (up to a certain point at least) to earn more money if needed. But typically, the ability to earn more ended when you reached the 40-hour mark each week.

As our business grew and became profitable, I could work fewer hours at my nursing job and more hours on our business. I was able to transition my mindset and not only clearly see the benefits of us working together for the life we were creating, but also the direct impact it had on the ability to be there more for our kids and family.

The flexibility we had because we worked for ourselves, the ease of going on a school field trip, staying home with a sick kid, visiting our family and kids in Florida or planning a vacation around nothing more than our business schedule made it all worth it.

I am so thankful that I could convert my "work hard for someone else as an employee" mentality to an entrepreneur mindset.

We truly do work well together, and our journey and vision have always been forward thinking, never looking backward."

–Cathy Taylor

It's been estimated that 19 million of the 28+ million U.S. small businesses are owned by couples.

Working together as a couple in business can be challenging, if not impossible if you both haven't laid out basic ground rules prior to making that initial commitment. My wife and I have seen couples literally destroy their business—not to mention their relationship, marriage, and family—by not following the basic principles we will outline throughout this chapter.

I would suggest that if you are a couple thinking about working together, start by reviewing this chapter with one another. If you are currently working together, I would highly suggest you discuss this chapter together to make your life, marriage, and relationship less stressful.

1. First, you both need to enjoy being around each other ALL the time. Think about it: you wake up together, you work together, and you go to bed together—seven days a week, 24 hours a day, 365 days a year. When you work and operate your own business together, your business now becomes part of your daily life. It is part of your daily conversations, part of your entire family's life, and most importantly, part of your marriage.

2. Couples that work together need to balance their marriage with both work and family. It is vitally important to spend quality time together intimately and have alone time away from each other as well.

3. Before making the decision to own and operate a business together, communication and having a mutual respect for each other is imperative to being successful.

When my wife and I had our publishing business in the '90s, the company we represented at the time recognized that part of our overall success was that we worked so well together.

They asked if we would mind having a couple fly down for the day to speak with us about our business and how we worked together as a married couple with children.

We weren't even with the couple for an hour before we both looked at each other and knew they would never be successful in running a business together.

All the wife did was belittle and talk down to her husband; never complimenting or saying anything positive to, or about him. As the couple left our office, they were arguing about responsibilities they would need to undertake in working together and what roles each would not be willing to assume.

They didn't have a single positive thing to say about each other the entire time they were with us that day.

4. Part of working together is clearly defining the responsibilities, expectations, and roles you will each be responsible for. After having this conversation, it is important not to overstep on those defined roles.

Each of you has strengths and areas where you excel that would best benefit your business and working relationship. I'm not saying you shouldn't take time to understand how to do the other responsibilities, but you will need to respect what the other is doing and let them do their job, so you can grow your business together.

My wife and I often tell couples jokingly that: "I did everything she didn't want to do and she did everything I didn't want to do."

However, that fact remains true today! At the end of the day, we both complement each other as a couple under the defined roles we were each responsible for.

5. It's important to remember that everyone (employees, contractors, customers, guests, patients, vendors, etc.) are watching you run your business together as a married couple. It is critical that you do not talk down to one another, embarrass each other, or argue in front of others.

You both should be setting an example for everyone to see. If you have a disagreement, go away from your business somewhere to talk it out and don't raise your voices. Keep in mind that it's not just your business partner you are talking to—it's your spouse; the person you love and are spending the rest of your life with.

"Having mutual respect is critical to the long-term success of working and growing your business together as a married couple."

6. As outlined in the points above, it is also important that there isn't a power struggle to be the boss or micromanage your spouse's responsibilities. You need to trust and believe in them, knowing that they are capable. Remember, you are working as a team—not as an individual.

Again, this comes down to having mutual respect and willingness to work together—all while supporting and motivating each other.

Years ago, I gave my wife a sign that I purchased at a store while shopping with my daughter.

I OWN the COMPANY and HE works for ME."

My wife still has that sign behind her desk all these years later. When you are comfortable in your marriage and working relationship, you can't get caught up in who is in charge.

You need to understand that you both have your own set of responsibilities and things that you do best and that it takes both of you to run a successful business together.

7. Transparency in all financial decisions is critical. It is important to agree on all financial decisions as a couple when taking on debt, vendors, purchases, leases, acquisitions, etc. Both of you need to understand how to read a P & L statement.

   Just as in marriage, the number one cause of stress in business is money. It's important—or rather, it is imperative—to go into your working partnership together with a clear understanding of where and how the money is and will be spent.

8. Working together allows both of you to regularly set new goals—both personally and for the growth and vision of

your business. It also allows you to celebrate successes and milestones together. Remember, not all couples are lucky enough to be able to both work and go home together every day.

9. As you work together with your spouse while raising a family, your children are exposed to your level of commitment, work ethic, and the struggles you face.

   This is something most children would never have had the ability to be exposed to or experience otherwise. Your kids will have a far greater appreciation for their parents' accomplishments, as they have witnessed your hard work and dedication to success firsthand.

10. Just as you would in a marriage, you need to be cautious about what you share with your friends, business acquaintances, parents, and especially extended family.

    Because it is such a balancing act trying to juggle marriage, children, business, family, and commitments, oftentimes the lines can get blurry.

    Remember to protect the privacy of your marriage and business by refraining from negative conversations around others—especially friends and family—about your day-to-day business challenges. Once either of you shares information with people outside your marriage, it can open the door to resentment and judgment from others.

11. You also have the ability to participate together in charitable foundations, fundraisers, and sponsorships with your business, as well as having the time to help and mentor others in need.

12. Finally, working together gives you flexibility, not just in your marriage, but in raising your children. It is much easier to be involved with your kids' events when they are younger, as you have flexibility in your schedule that many people do not have. You can plan times to visit with your family, grandchildren, and friends, and take well-deserved vacations as you both work around your busy but flexible schedule together.

> **"It's amazing what you can accomplish in life—what goals you can achieve and obstacles you can get through—when you work together as a married couple, not against each other."**

8 SUSTAINABILITY

WHETHER YOU ARE an executive representing a major corporation, department manager or an entrepreneur running your own business or franchise, you want to know your efforts and the business model you represent is sustainable long-term.

I have always had the philosophy to lead by example, which I will expand on later in the book.

I always wanted my team to know that to be successful in business you must be 110% committed to anything you set out to accomplish. If someone wants to enter your space (the type of specific business you represent) and become a serious competitor, regardless of the industry you are in, they will need to do everything you are currently doing in your business and more in order to be successful. I also strongly believe that if you are running your own business as your primary source of income, you need to be working your business full-time, not part-time. Your results are the direct reflection of not just your commitment, but the work you put into growing your business. As the saying goes, "Part-time efforts equal part-time results; full-time efforts equal full-time results."

> "There are only two options regarding commitment. You're either IN or, you're OUT. There is no such thing as life in-between."
>
> -Pat Riley

To truly be successful as an entrepreneur, you need to be all in—not doing the hokey pokey with one foot in and one foot out! This lack of commitment alone will cause you and your business to be enormously vulnerable, as well as affect your sustainability long-term.

This is where keeping your "finger on the pulse of your business" plays a critical role in long-term sustainability.

As we built our publishing business early on, I took the approach that I would need to dominate our sphere of influence. With that, I was prepared to do what no one else was willing to do, including outworking anyone I felt would be a potential threat in the area and space that I represented.

As an entrepreneur, there is always a concern about someone trying to invade your space.

So, I'll ask you entrepreneurs, franchise and business owners out there: are you doing what no one else is willing to do? Are you willing to do whatever it takes to make it more challenging for a competitor to come in and take some of your market share or business away from you?

If not, WHY? More importantly, what makes you think your business is sustainable long-term?

Here are a few things I put in place early on that I felt took the edge off that concern. If these suggestions are implemented, you will feel more comfortable with the businesses you operate, manage or control.

> **Are you willing to do what no one else is willing to do to be successful in business today?"**

#1 | UNDERSTAND YOUR INDUSTRY

Knowledge is power. Understanding your industry and competition is critical to staying ahead of the game and is a large part of positioning yourself to win in business. Remember, being average today will not cut it anymore; to be intentionally successful you need to stand out by differentiating yourself from others.

Do your homework; research and become an expert and solution provider in your industry. This will give you a winning edge over your competition.

If you don't understand every inch of your business—not just locally, regionally, nationally or even globally—you are leaving yourself and your business extremely vulnerable.

#2 | ATTENTION TO DETAIL

In the industry I represented, having high attention to detail was critical because of the high-end printing product we published. With that said, this can also be seen in the visual appeal, content, links, and accuracy of the information and images showcased on your website, blog, social/digital platforms and marketing utilized to represent your brand. This rings true regardless of what type of industry you are in.

Signage, banners, brochures, menus, and retail positioning of products and services are also a huge part of attention to detail. As a business owner, you should be dotting the I's and crossing the T's in EVERYTHING you do to run your company.

"It's all about the DETAILS, period."

When shortcuts are taken, they will usually come back to haunt you for the rest of your life. Attention to detail is vitally important in every business and industry.

Don't think your customers, guests, clients, prospects or competition won't take notice of the small things you could be doing but are choosing not to.

"The worst thing is to have someone study what you should be doing but choose not to, then come in and duplicate your business, doing a better job due to your complacency."

Attention to detail also applies to little things such as your email signature. It drives me nuts when I am corresponding with someone, and they reply by email from their tablet or mobile device with no signature—sometimes without even a name at the end of their email response! If I want to call them back, I don't have their number. This is not the way you want to represent yourself professionally.

When businesses do not pay attention to the details and presentation of their products or services, the reputation of their brand is significantly impacted.

An example of one simple detail that can have a huge impact is creating professional stationery for yourself or your business. Everyone likes to be acknowledged or thanked personally, whether they are a client, customer or guest. It's the little things that make a big difference and go a long way in creating incredible customer relationships.

#3 | CREATING A SYSTEM FOR EVERYTHING

Every business, whether large or small, needs to have systems in place—and implemented—to be successful. In the businesses we have operated over the years, we made sure we were creating systems and processes for everything—down to how to set up a signature on your mobile device (as mentioned previously).

Franchises build their entire infrastructure on having their franchisees follow their proven system of success.

As I have mentioned before, not following the system in your business or the company you represent is like not breathing air. If you have a small business, have you created systems that will allow you to run your business as you grow and scale your brand and organization?

Can your business operate smoothly when you are unavailable to answer questions that could have immediately been answered if you had the right systems in place?

Systems also allow you to duplicate your business while keeping your brand consistent as you grow.

I have watched many businesses struggle due to a lack of organization. That said, having systems set up and not enforcing those systems will only contribute to the challenges, struggles and frustrations you will be confronted with as a business owner.

#4 | TRAINING

Training your team is vital to building a sustainable business. When we started to expand our media business in 2006, we created a training manual. Over the years, this manual grew from 40 to over 500 pages. For years, we used the training manual to review all segments of building a successful business. We made sure to include all the mistakes that were previously made, in order to help prevent those same mistakes from happening again.

The training manual also included all the systems of duplication and processes that would keep individuals representing the brand on track. Today the 500+ page training manual has been replaced by a secure online portal. Every time we encounter a question, problem or solution, change a process or create marketing images, we create a reference guide broken down into a variety of categories.

Today the reference guides cover 98% of the systems and processes in duplicating the brand nationally—regardless of the geographical area.

What's nice about the reference guides today is that they can easily be updated as technology changes and the systems are modified, unlike the previously printed training manuals. The secure online portal also includes conference call audio, video, and resource links.

In your organization, have you created a training manual or online portal to help guide your team to represent your business as it grows properly, scales and expands?

In addition to the training manual, are you providing real-time training with all new team members representing your company?

Whether you are a single operation or have multiple locations, communication with your team is critical.

Building a strong organization is all about building strong relationships. This starts with the people who are representing you, your brand and your business.

Bringing in speakers, experts in your field and professionals to teach, share experiences and instill motivation is also important in growing your organization.

Consistently collaborating with your team, sharing ideas, goals, and visions is critical in creating a culture for growing a sustainable business long-term.

#5 | COMPLACENCY

Throughout this book, I have shared experiences and struggles that my wife and I faced early on when moving across the US to launch our first magazine in the early '90s. When we initially entered the market, there was a direct competitor representing a national franchise brand. They had been in the market for eight years and had a decent foothold in the area—or at least that was what I thought at the time.

Part of my strategy in going against the competitor was utilizing the intangibles as reviewed in Chapter One. I had the belief, passion, posture, and relatability, and I was growing every day in further understanding the product and brand I was representing.

I quickly picked up that my competitor had taken their finger off the pulse of their business. They forgot all the hard work they originally did to start up their company, and they lost sight of their why and purpose in running a successful business. They became complacent and greedy in the brand they represented, even though they were part of a national franchise.

They lost their passion for running their business, lost their relatability in customer service and stopped creating value in the services they provided.

With that said, my competitor shut down eight months after we launched our first magazine in 1994. Overnight they literally disappeared, leaving my future clients deeply disappointed and skeptical and wondering if I was going to do the same thing.

When I think of complacency, I think about losing the burning desire and passion to succeed intentionally.

Personally, I attribute a big part of why businesses fail to the entrepreneur or business owner becoming complacent, greedy, and losing the passion to succeed. They have taken their finger off the pulse of their business, which in the end can cost them everything.

#6 | IMPORTANCE OF CUSTOMER SERVICE

Taking the time to listen to your customers, clients, guests, and patients regarding their concerns—and understanding what they want—is critical to creating a sustainable business model.

Your customers need to be your number one priority ALL the time, NOT just some of the time.

> "Building a connection with your customers is critical to running a successful, sustainable business."

I would strongly suggest taking the time and making it a priority to have incredible customer service and develop lasting relationships with your clients if you want a sustainable business model.

In the retail business, it was all about customer service. Maybe that is why it was so natural for me to build relationships with my clients when I entered the publishing industry. Those relationships proved to be crucial during a difficult period early on.

1. After being in Portland for just two years, I got sick—really, really sick. I was hospitalized several times over the next few months. I had to have a specific procedure done, and there was a 3% chance of having a reaction. Of course, I was one of the 3%.

   In the publishing industry, it was all about deadlines, ad submission, design, and circulation. Guess who helped my wife put together our next publication while I was in the hospital? Our clients! They came together and pitched in; some of them coming to our home office, working long hours with my wife. Remember—our home office was in the living and dining room at that point. Despite that fact, they did whatever was needed to get the next issue submitted to our printer.

As I reflect on that situation, I realize that our clients were also our friends. Not necessarily friends who hang out together, but friends who cared about us and the products and services they purchased from us. They understood that we didn't have any family in the area, and they knew the sacrifices and commitments we made to be there. They also appreciated that we were always looking out for their best interests in order to help them grow their own businesses. This is why sharing your story is so important in the process of developing and growing your business.

In every publication my wife and I have personally operated together over the years, we feel that there have been several important factors in establishing long-term relationships with clients. These include integrity, credibility, transparency, authenticity and creating and capturing value in what you are doing.

2. My wife and I had just come back from a national conference where we were awarded "Publisher of the Year." The following weekend, I was out running some errands. When we met up later in the day, I was completely oblivious to the fact that my wife was having a surprise birthday party for me. When I walked in, all my clients were there shouting "Happy Birthday!"

These were clients who had been with us since day one and were major players in the market we represented. They took time out of their busy schedule to come out on a Saturday afternoon and celebrate with us. It was awesome seeing the relationships we had created by simply treating our clients like we would want to be treated.

I remember sharing one of the awards we had just received with our clients and hearing their genuine appreciation for us and what we were doing in the market. Looking back, I see that these are the memories that made all the struggles, disappointments and challenges we encountered early on worth it.

SIX RULES TO ALWAYS FOLLOW IN BUSINESS

RULE **1** CUSTOMER SERVICE

RULE **4** CLIENT INTERACTIONS

RULE **2** PRODUCT PLACEMENT

RULE **5** DON'T GET GREEDY

RULE **3** BRAND AWARENESS

RULE **6** RULE #1

Today, too many organizations and businesses have lost sight of just how important customer service and client relationships are to the long-term growth and sustainability of their business.

I teach entrepreneurs from growing businesses not to treat their clients, customers, guests, patients or employees like numbers. I encourage them to develop relationships that are a true representation of character and transparency of their brand—and of course, the individual behind the brand.

Most importantly, if you tell someone you will do something, make sure you follow through. The worst thing you can ever do is to over-promise and under-deliver.

If you watch successful businesses grow today, you will likely see the following characteristics displayed. They are all providing incredible customer service and focusing on building long-term relationships. Additionally, they are presenting themselves with transparency, relatability and professionalism every day of the week—not just a few.

The following example is a true testament to customer service.

Our dentist is incredible. He has an awesome practice, is always relatable, is passionate about his profession and truly cares about his patients. He always asks how your day is going, how your family is doing and picks up on your last conversation—regardless of the time that has passed since your last visit.

I really don't know how he does it with all the patients he sees! One day I asked his wife, who manages the office, how he remembers the conversations he has with his patients. She replied that he uses a program (which would be similar to a CRM) where he places all his clinical notes of the patients he sees that day. The morning before seeing his patients he reviews all his prior notes, thus being able to pick up on the last conversation.

This is why having a CRM is critical in running your business!

In all my years of going to the dentist, he is the only one who has ever taken the time to call us at home personally. Every time he performs any type of procedure, big or small, our phone would always ring around 7 p.m.—yes, every time.

He stays well into the evening to make those phone calls personally, all while logging in his notes from that day.

I admire how he represents his practice with integrity, professionalism, sincerity, compassion, and empathy.

He goes the extra mile to make sure he is providing you with the highest level of care that he can because at the end of the day he truly cares—that's what makes him intentionally successful in operating his practice.

> **We believe that customer service shouldn't be just a department: it should be the entire company."**
>
> *–Tony Hsieh, CEO of Zappos*

#7 | DON'T BECOME GREEDY

Greed can destroy your business, regardless of the industry you are in. This can be seen by the following:

1. Employee morale and interactions become affected.
2. Total lack of customer service becomes obvious.
3. Making the business all about the money. Looking for more ways to raise pricing, thus not creating any value in your product, brand or the services provided.
4. Making bad personal decisions that ultimately and directly affect your business and the personnel who represent your business.
5. Taking advantage of employees, clients, customers, and guests.
6. Not willing to reinvest back into their business.
7. Not having the willingness to help, lead and mentor others.
8. Lack of relatability and empathy.

9. Not operating by your mission statement or the culture you initially outlined in launching your business.

10. Not having a true purpose in running your business apart from simply making money.

#8 | THINKING PAST TOMORROW

I have a saying that goes, "It's not about what you are doing today, it's about what you will be doing next year, five years from now and more that will position you to win in business." Too many entrepreneurs are so focused on today; they lose sight of the bigger picture tomorrow.

> "Don't be afraid of change ... Be afraid of NOT changing."

In the professional world, you must stay ahead of the game. Part of that includes technology and being open and willing to change as technology changes.

A lot of business owners are not willing to invest in this area because they have been successful without it up to this point, or simply because of the costs involved.

What they don't understand is the invaluable benefits technology can bring to their business. These benefits include creating efficiency, inventory management, customer relationship management, project management, reporting, accounting, training, design, lead generation, email campaigns, web, digital and social platforms just to name a few. Implementing these tools and applications will take your business to the next level.

> "As the saying goes, if you continue to do what you've always done, you'll continue to get what you always got."

#9 | MANAGING YOUR EXPENSES

As you run your business, you need to be aware of your expenses constantly. This includes looking out for ways to cut costs without jeopardizing your story, integrity, performance, customer service, quality, purchasing, and overall efficiency. It's also important to consult your accountant regarding the latest tax laws.

Ways to cut costs may include:

- Buying a building vs. leasing space in a building
- Switching to a VOIP phone system vs. landline phone system
- Annually reviewing credit card processing rates and their integration with your systems
- Buying equipment vs. leasing
- Payroll services and online time clock vs. manual
- Consistently evaluating mailing and shipping needs, just to name a few

I love the following story my daughter-in-law shared with me. She managed a law firm overseeing the administration and was placed in charge of looking at ways to make the firm more efficient—thus cutting expenses.

She presented a simple way to save thousands of dollars a year by switching from a postage meter to an online postage service.

The partners of the firm were all aboard and excited about this specific change, but when the change was explained to the staff, there was total resistance. Why?

The staff didn't want to re-learn a new process that they had become comfortable with over the years. They didn't embrace change as being efficient or cost-cutting, even though it was explained in detail how it would make their job much easier. Frankly, they were lazy—unwilling to take the time to understand that this specific change would ultimately be more efficient and save a huge amount of money for the firm.

When you implement something new in your business, it's important to make sure you know everything about the change before rolling it out.

Use language your team can relate to and explain why the change is necessary. Take the time to properly train them, and always be available for questions and feedback. This allows your team to feel comfortable in the decision you have just executed.

It's human nature to resist change, especially when it comes to technology, so have some empathy when rolling out these changes and remember: it's in the best interest of your company's future.

After all, you do have the final say in what changes will be made in your business, and if you feel it is in the best interest of the company, then the staff will need to conform to the new changes implemented.

#10 | HAVING THE RIGHT TEAM

I recently had a great conversation with a business owner who wanted to expand their company, but I sensed concern throughout our discussions about creating the right team.

When they asked me what the hardest part of expanding your business is, I could only respond with one word: people.

You can be in the best location, represent an awesome product or service, and have all the resources in place, however, if you don't have the right person trained to run your business or manage your team, you will quickly end up with huge regret. Not only will you need to replace them fast, but you will be cleaning up the mess they created along the way. It's important always to remember that your team—the individuals representing you, your company and your brand—are crucial to the ultimate success and culture of your business.

#11 | CREATE YOUR STORY WITH AUTHENTICITY

Creating your story is what truly defines who you are as a brand, organization or company.

Businesses should always promote their story in their marketing, on their website and in their physical locations. Your story allows you to educate the consumer while being relatable and authentic. This applies whether you are just starting a business, expanding your current company or increasing your brand awareness. Your story allows you to do just that—tell your story.

Telling your unique story might involve sharing the following:

- The hardships you've encountered as you've built your brand
- The history and timeline of your business, including any acquisitions or mergers that took place
- What makes your brand unique in the industry you represent
- Your company culture and mission statement
- Photos of your team
- Share what makes your business stand out from others in your industry
- Video of your business, customers, and team
- Testimonials.

Remember: your story is an important part of the foundation of your business.

> **"Never make a point without a story, never tell a story without a point."**
>
> -Les Brown

When my wife and I moved from Florida to Oregon to start our publishing business, I shared our story for years as we expanded our magazine titles. Clients respected the fact that my wife and I took a chance to start a business in a place so far from family and friends.

Your story is a huge part of the transparency, authenticity, history, and culture of growing your business, so don't be afraid to share it. As they say… the best story wins.

#12 | MARKETING & ADVERTISING

In every business advertising and marketing are extremely important in growing your brand. With that said, if you are a smaller company, it is wise to hire an expert to assist in your marketing/advertising designs. As you grow your business, you can bring this process in-house—even if it's just part-time. Your graphic artist is a critical part of growing and professionally representing your business through marketing and promotional branding.

It's amazing what a graphic artist can do to help your business—not just with the look of your website, but in your everyday marketing that directly reflects your brand and how your business looks overall.

The colors you choose in your marketing are what subconsciously create a feeling, perception, and attraction to your brand, product or service. Your fonts and typeface are critically important in allowing an audience of all ages to be able to identify with your message/content. Remember, it is important to "keep it simple." You have just a few seconds to pique someone's interest—are you using eye-catching photos and clear, concise verbiage to get your point across quickly?

As with any advertising, being consistent in your marketing plan is vitally important to get your message out there. However, as a business owner, you should not place all your ad dollars in one specific form of advertising. Spreading your marketing out and utilizing a variety of media platforms will allow you to target your audiences in multiple ways.

FORMS OF MARKETING/ADVERTISING:

1. Print Advertising
   a. Magazine
   b. Newspaper
   c. Direct Mail Marketing
   d. Flyers, Brochures, Inserts
2. Online/Digital Advertising
   a. Website
   b. Social Media
   c. Video
   d. Email Campaigns
   e. Mobile
   f. Blog
3. Placement Branding
   a. Retail/Grocery/Restaurant
   b. Movie Theaters
   c. TV/Movies
4. Broadcasting
   a. Local Radio
   b. Local TV Networks
   c. Local Cable/Satellite Networks
   d. National/Regional Cable/Satellite Networks
   e. Public Service Broadcasting

5. Outdoor Placement Advertising
   a. Still Billboards
   b. Digital Billboards
6. General
   a. Special Events Promoting the Brand, Product or Service
   b. Networking Events
   c. Sponsorship Events
   d. Promotional Marketing

MARKETING STRATEGIES TO CONSIDER

1. Marketing gives your business a boost of brand awareness, creating credibility in your message and boosting your reputation.

2. Marketing allows you to tell your story and get the word out about what you do.

3. Marketing increases your social media exposure, which drives targeted traffic to your website and boosts your SEO.

4. Marketing in conjunction with your social media consistently reminds your customers to follow you by using hashtags, tweets, and posts promoting events, sales, products and services you are introducing.

5. Marketing builds brand loyalty and retention.

6. Marketing targets the clientele you want as customers.

7. Marketing allows you to increase sales.

8. Marketing retains existing customers and consistently informs them based on the time of year, promotion, etc.

9. Marketing allows you to compete with all types of businesses while differentiating your brand from the others.

10. Marketing allows you to stay in control of your targeted audience and understand your business better. This process also allows you to collect data and measure analytics based on the information you are receiving such as email addresses. Email campaigns for businesses are very successful if properly and professionally designed for promotions and brand recognition.

Coming from a niche magazine background, magazine advertising not only differentiates you and your brand from others including colleagues, it is targeted, relevant, credible and lasting. Images tell the story with emotional connections, drive both web, social/digital exposure, enhance ROI and drive sales and lead generation.

MARKETING 101 FOR NEW BUSINESS OWNERS

If you are a business just getting started, here are a few things I would suggest to kick off your marketing and branding strategies.

1. When you come up with the name of your business, make sure you select a domain name that matches or comes close to your business name. While I was writing this book, I was instructed by my publisher to come up with a website representing my name. Since there was a current author who was also named Brad Taylor, I became "The Brad Taylor," while also securing the domain name to match. In business, you need to be creative in your marketing.

2. Have a logo professionally designed—it will be placed consistently on all your marketing (web, social, digital, print, direct mail etc.).

3. Choose your color theme and fonts that will be consistent in ALL your marketing.

4. Remember, the size of your text needs to be readable to all ages. Don't use text so small you need a magnifying glass to read what you have written!

5. Create a "tagline" that describes your business and keep it down to no more than 10 words if at all possible. Your tagline is a snapshot of your business and what you stand for.

6. Create a mission/culture statement of your business and use it on your website and in a brochure with your story.

7. Identify what types of social media will best target your audience, and design with the theme outlined in 1 through 4.

8. Anything you are writing or creating for marketing purposes needs to be proofed by multiple individuals. Spelling errors and distorted images make you and your brand look very unprofessional—remember to keep it simple and clean.

9. Have fun with your marketing; be creative and think outside the box like I did in creating "The Brad Taylor."

10. There are so many promotional branding websites out there today (also known as promotional swag). Pick a few items that you can place your logo and website on. These items vary from seasonal to everyday things including pens, mugs, letter openers, shirts, tumblers, all-purpose bags, etc.

> " A man who stops advertising
> to save money is like a man who
> stops a clock to save time."
>
> -Henry Ford

#13 | SOCIAL MEDIA

I will keep this short since I have already addressed social media in the previous chapters. Why am I even mentioning social media under sustainability? Because it holds massive potential for destruction.

Regardless of how large or small your position or company is, what you post on social media platforms (and the internet in general) can literally sabotage your business or livelihood overnight.

Careers and businesses have been ruined by a single tweet or post in the one second it took to hit the submit button.

There are certain things you should never discuss while running or managing your social media platforms—period!

I have personally witnessed employees not getting their dream job, executives of major companies losing their positions and business owners sabotaging their livelihood through social media. This happens by overtly discussing political views, religious beliefs and posting/sharing inappropriate messages and tweets on social media platforms.

Be cautious about what you post and share (due to the threads created). This doesn't apply to just social media, but the internet as a whole—these posts will, at some point, come back to haunt you for life.

It is simply not worth losing everything you worked so hard to accomplish from just one click of your computer keyboard, tablet or mobile device.

> **Social media is not your diary, keep your posts positive, not negative."**
> *-Ashley T. Hagen*

9 IMPORTANCE OF LEADERSHIP

"The most powerful leadership tool you have is your own personal example."

-John Wooden

lead•er•ship

noun: the position or function of a leader, a person who guides or directs a group

LEADERSHIP IS A KEY component of intentional success and is imperative in order to take your business or organization to the next level.

In my opinion, leadership is something you need to earn and should never be taken for granted or expected. Leadership is not a position or a title; it is simply leading by example.

We have all encountered—or maybe we have been—the opposite of a great leader. For lack of better words, let's call the person a "poor leader." You know, the type of person who sits on their high horse, barking orders at the people below them.

This type of leadership is a) not sustainable; b) not efficient, and c) does not empower people to succeed.

Being a true leader is being a great leader, which allows you to focus on significance rather than success and purpose rather than just numbers. A great leader is willing to listen, professionally responds to situations instead of reacting to them, and encourages others rather than micromanaging them.

I would suggest taking a good look at the table below, and asking yourself the following:

"Am I a 'great leader,' or am I being a 'poor leader'?"

I am constantly asked how I still have a passion for business, and what keeps me going after all these years. This question can be answered two-fold:

1. I think it starts by having sincerity, transparency, empathy, gratitude and the ability to take responsibility for your actions in what you do in life.

2. With that said, I also enjoy helping people succeed in business, inspiring them, motivating them and truly caring about their overall success and dreams.

In running a variety of companies and businesses over the years, I have learned to put people first. This comes by listening to their ideas, suggestions, and thoughts with the intention of understanding their needs and desire to succeed. It is important to treat them as an individual and more importantly as part of the team—not just a number within your organization.

I have always believed that you should treat your team, clients, customers, and guests as you would want to be treated. As shared in previous chapters, I was deeply impacted by the way the owners

GREAT LEADER		POOR LEADER
FOCUSED ON SIGNIFICANCE	VS	**FOCUSED** JUST ON SUCCESS
LEADS WITH A VISION	VS	**FOCUSED** ON JUST THE NUMBERS
ENCOURAGES OTHERS	VS	**MICROMANAGES** OTHERS
LEARNS FROM THEIR MISTAKES	VS	**FEAR** OF MAKING MISTAKES
GROWS PERSONALLY	VS	**KNOWS** EVERYTHING
LEADS BY EXAMPLE	VS	**UNWILLING** TO GET HANDS DIRTY
GIVES CREDIT TO OTHERS	VS	**TAKES** ALL THE CREDIT
LISTENS 80% OF THE TIME	VS	**TALKS** 80% OF THE TIME
TAKES RISKS	VS	**FEARS** RISKING AND FAILING
CREATES CHANGE	VS	**RESISTS** CHANGE
TAKES FULL RESPONSIBILITY	VS	**ALWAYS** BLAMING OTHERS
SENSE OF GRATITUDE	VS	**SENSE** OF ENTITLEMENT
MENTORS OTHERS TO SUCCEED	VS	**WORRIED** ONLY ABOUT THEMSELVES
DOES NOT HOLD A GRUDGE	VS	**HOLDS A GRUDGE** OR RESENTMENT FOR OTHERS
EMPATHY; SINCERE FEELINGS	VS	**APATHY;** LACK OF INTEREST
PLANS FOR THE FUTURE	VS	**WORRIED** JUST ABOUT TODAY

of the drug store reached out and invested in me when I was an impressionable 18-year-old.

This was something that happened 40+ years ago, but even now as you read or listen to the audio of this book, I still take time to reflect on that specific instance and how it shaped the rest of my life as both a mentor and an entrepreneur.

With that said, you can't save everyone. It's hard to help someone succeed if they are not willing to listen to and follow the vision, culture, and systems your organization has put into place.

As a leader, your goal is to do your best in mentoring, coaching and empowering your team. Unfortunately, there will occasionally be someone who will still buck the system and the advice you give them.

For those who choose not to be team players, you need to immediately cut them loose—as negativity alone can become a toxic virus within any organization if left unattended.

One thing a mentor said to me years ago that I will never forget relates to responding to issues that need to be immediately handled.

> " Be cautious as to how you respond to someone, it's like squeezing the toothpaste out of the tube—once it's out, you will never be able to put it back in."

This can be applied to both business and personal relationships. That saying above involves the words you choose to use, your actions and the tone of your voice. It is better to take the time to reflect and think about the situation that just occurred before you respond rather than responding immediately. Words, whether spoken or via email or text, should be carefully thought out and composed. Email and text can easily be misinterpreted; you do not want to have regret down the road for the words you used.

I'm a big believer in picking up the phone, or better yet, meeting in person—never hiding behind an email or text message.

Lastly, a great leader will not hold a grudge—or have resentment with thoughts of revenge, when they have been placed in unfortunate situations. Holding a grudge will only consume you, your judgment toward others and the individuals around you. An example of this was in chapter six when we were forced to hire a litigation attorney. We personally knew the parties involved, and at the end, no one walked away the winner; it just destroyed relationships. Since that specific situation, my faith, along with my leadership, has allowed me to move on and not hold a grudge or have resentment with the parties involved; it is a path not many others would have chosen.

> **A great leader will not hold a grudge or have resentment toward others."**

Over the years, I have had individuals come to me with advice they were given by a coach they had worked with. They then asked me for my thoughts or advice about the suggestions they were given to implement.

First, let me say up front that I am in no way against working with a professional coach. Business coaches are incredible at keeping the individuals and organizations they are working with on task, accountable, engaged, motivated, and focused on their ultimate goals and vision, both personally and professionally.

I just want to make that clear before I continue.

After I asked a series of questions related to the conversations they had with their coach, I realized that some of the suggestions they were advised to implement would significantly impact their business, their employees, their family, and livelihood. More importantly, their coach never truly took the time to understand completely their business or to consult their accountant for more information.

When I asked the individual about the level of experience the business coach had, they were not able to answer the question completely. They had met through a friend and felt that the coach seemed easy to talk with and was affordable.

This is where the red flag comes up for me: the person they are paying to seek advice from has never operated a business before. They have never experienced the ups and downs of business ownership or even held a leadership role in running a company. Worse yet, they have never put up any of their own money to start a business, sacrificing everything to succeed—so how are they giving advice to a business owner?

If you are looking for a coach to work with, someone to advise you in your business ventures—over and above your accountant, financial adviser and attorney—make sure the person you are hiring has either walked the walk in an executive role in running a company or operated their own business venture. No one will truly understand and appreciate what you are going through and be able to professionally advise you if they haven't experienced both the successes and failures of running a business themselves.

> **"** A mentor is someone who sees more talent and ability within you, than you see in yourself, and helps bring it out of you."
>
> *-Bob Proctor*

CHEERLEADER VS. COACH

I have heard this expression shared in many different ways over the years: "coach vs. cheerleader." I love to use this analogy as I advise ceo's, business owners and department managers on struggles they may be having.

When I am working with individuals or teams to help them grow their business, I am not there to be their cheerleader. I am there to support their vision and empower them, but at the same time, I am there to let them know what they may be doing wrong, get them back on track and coach them to be successful in running their organization.

I truly feel that honesty is what people need to hear when they are seeking you out for professional advice.

I will flat out tell people: "I'm not here to be your cheerleader; I'm here to be your coach. I'll be the one to tell you what you don't want to hear. However, I am also the one that is looking out for your best interest all along the way. I want you to succeed in accomplishing your goals and dreams intentionally."

Don't get me wrong; everyone needs encouragement and positive motivation. I know I sure did when I was getting started in business! But, if all I am doing is telling them they are awesome, endorsing and saying what they want to hear and cheering them on the path they are currently on ... then all I am doing is setting them up for failure down the road.

A great leader will take the time to listen with both ears and ask lots and lots of questions. At the same time, they will challenge and push individuals out of their comfort zone in order to accomplish their goals and vision.

So, if I was your coach, I would tell you that I am NOT here to be your cheerleader—you can get that so-called motivation from your family and friends.

I'm here to challenge you and tell you what your family and friends may not be willing to tell you out of fear of hurting your feelings or crushing your dreams. I'm here to push you to be the very best you can be in both your personal and professional life, while also utilizing the twelve intangibles of success as outlined in Chapter One.

My goal is to take you out of your comfort zone so that moving forward, you will have intentional success in anything you put your mind to.

It's amazing that 50% of the advice I give entrepreneurs incorporates chapter seven of this book, "Working with Your Spouse." In this situation, my wife and I can mentor the couple, working together to address the problems they may be having or struggling with while being relatable all along the way as a couple ourselves that still work together all these years later. We have a unique perspective and understanding of what it takes to be committed to both marriage and family, as well as to the running, working and managing a successful business over many years.

In my experience over the last 40+ years, people want to know that their leader is not so far above them that they can't understand, relate to or value the task or position they hold within the company.

That is why, in every company I ever owned, I wanted my employees and the individuals representing my companies to see it wasn't beneath me to do the same things I would ask of them. Whether it was unloading a truck, cleaning the bathroom, stocking shelves, taking out the garbage, working long hours, weekends or making the calls that created results; it was all part of my job description as a great leader who was leading by example.

> "The most powerful leadership tool you have is your own personal example."
>
> -John Wooden

I also understand that this is not always feasible with larger companies. However, the leader, when possible, should periodically visit the various departments of their business, representing the success of the company and meeting the individuals working in those departments on a consistent basis. This includes sharing the vision, inspiration, empowerment, achievements, and culture the company represents.

In the case of smaller companies, lead by example and don't be afraid to get your hands dirty and spend time out in the field with your team whenever possible.

As our publishing company grew over the years, our publishers appreciated that my wife and I had previously operated magazines ourselves.

This allowed us to relate to our team about what to do and not do in order to be intentionally successful. This application also allowed us to lead by example as we shared stories relating to the specific situations they were encountering at the time; we were able to share our own experiences and how we learned from them.

This also showed our team that we weren't afraid to get our hands dirty. This is something that goes a long way—not just in creating credibility and trust. It instills relatability, authenticity, and empathy in running a successful company.

> " What you do has a far greater
> impact than what you say."
> -Stephen Covey

THE PULSE OF YOUR BUSINESS

You have heard me mention the phrase "keeping your finger on the pulse of your business" in other parts of the book, and here is what it boils down to. As the leader of a company, whether you are running a major corporation or a small business with one employee, you need to know what's going on in your business or organization at all times.

Part of this has to do with the communication layers (management) within your organization, your team, your systems, processes and knowing your financial numbers on an ongoing basis—not just once a year. It is especially important to be open to suggestions, all while never putting your business on autopilot or in jeopardy.

"If you think you are the smartest person in the room, you're in the wrong room."

I always seek out information from my team, letting them know that their thoughts, insights, and suggestions are very important to me.

Remember the story in Chapter Seven about complacency, where the franchisee took their finger off the pulse of their business—which ultimately allowed their business to fail?

This exact thing happens to other businesses, every single day. Whether the company grew too fast, didn't have the proper infrastructure or systems in place or the leadership of the company was just not there, it is easy to lose sight of what's happening in your business.

It is your job as the leader of the company, big or small, to know what's going on in your business. How are your employees treating your clients, your vendors, your guests, your customers and just as important—how are they treating fellow coworkers? How are they responding to stress in the workplace? Are they professionally representing your company, not just in person, but through the phone, email, etc.? Have you made unexpected visits, or better yet, have you sent secret shoppers into your retail or service locations?

If you are not on top of your business, you are in big trouble because at the end of the day, no one is looking out for your company's best interests better than you and your executive team.

10 TRUE INTENTIONAL SUCCESS

"True intentional success is never forgetting what got you started; always remembering the struggles, failures, frustrations, and adversities and learning from every mistake you have ever made."

FOR ME, INTENTIONAL success in life is not just about the money and the things that come with it.

Don't get me wrong; my wife and I have worked extremely hard to be where we are in life today. However, success to us is also about family, health, spirituality, gratitude, priorities, purpose, significance, humility, happiness and having discretionary time—which has become a precious commodity, especially as we get older.

Intentional success is also measured in the lives you have helped touch and change because of the opportunities, guidance and mentoring you have given.

Remember the kind words of Tomas Martinez III in the forward of this book? He is just one example of a life changed through following the intangibles of success; as his success is ultimately my intentional success in life!

Here is another great success story from our friends Herman and Diane:

"We are successful today in operating our business because of the quality time we were able to spend with Brad and Cathy Taylor well over 20 years ago.

Brad and Cathy mentored us when we were just starting our business and didn't know the first thing about what we were doing.

Every time we were at a conference, we would try to spend time with them, listening to what they were doing and their words of wisdom and encouragement.

I remember Brad saying to me multiple times, "Herman, don't reinvent the wheel, just take one or two ideas back with you and implement them well."

And that's exactly what we did… If we ever had a problem, we could call Brad, and he would talk us through it. When we were finished, Brad always had a way of making us understand that the HUGE problem we were facing was actually very minor, and it could be controlled or changed very easily.

The one thing my wife and I learned very quickly was this: when Brad was talking, it was time to shut up and listen—your life was about to change for the better!

His experience, expertise, and friendship are invaluable. It is an honor to know them both as friends and mentors."

-Herman and Diane
Entrepreneurs

Successful people will give to others knowing that the others can't repay the favor, while also understanding it's just the right thing to do.

> **Change your focus from making money to serving more people. Serving more people makes the money come in."**
>
> *-Robert Kiyosaki*

True intentional success is never forgetting what got you started; always remembering the struggles, failures, frustrations, and adversities and learning from every mistake you have ever made.

In many ways, success is the sense of fulfillment that comes from your hard work and never giving up on your dreams and goals. This applies at any age, in both personal and professional settings.

After my wife and I began to have success, one of my goals was to one day write a book. Here I am, many years later, doing just that—accomplishing one of my goals!

In chapter one, I listed the twelve intangibles that will guide you in accomplishing anything you set out to pursue in life.

It doesn't matter if you are a student, stay-at-home parent, employee, executive, entrepreneur, business owner or just enjoying retirement life with your friends and family. Combining all twelve intangibles truly creates the formula for **Intentional Success**.

When you have Faith in your life… it creates Belief.

When you have Passion in your life… it creates Persistence

When you have Knowledge in your life… it creates Posture.

When you have Integrity in your life… it creates Leadership.

When you have Empathy in your life… it creates Relatability.

When you have a Goal in your life… it creates Balance.

Use this formula and share the meaning of **Intentional Success** with others…

Remember the time my father-in-law told my wife and me that we were going to fail and be back in Florida within a year because we decided to move across the United States to start a new business venture?

Today, when I bring this up to my father-in-law, he always responds jokingly by saying…

> " I just said that to motivate you
> to become successful."

But let me tell you: his tone, temperament and disappointment at the time were not motivating in any way, shape or form.

I have used my father-in-law as an example many times when speaking to audiences and groups. I've used him to demonstrate that even if someone doesn't support you initially, if you just stay true to your character, be patient and continue to communicate with sincerity, most will come around eventually. This is something my father-in-law did quickly as he watched my wife and I intentionally succeed in what we set out to accomplish over 25 years ago.

And this is where payback is so awesome.

When my father-in-law retired in 2007—after the dealership he worked for closed due to the economy—I decided to have my 50th Anniversary Corvette, with less than 2,500 miles, shipped from California to Florida. My father-in-law loved driving that car when he would come to visit us, so that was going to be my surprise—or should I say "payback"—to him.

I had the Corvette shipped to my friend's home in Florida for safekeeping until I arrived a month later. We strategically came up with a plan where my friend and his wife set up a time to meet my in-laws for dinner at a Japanese steakhouse. I surprised my father-in-law by driving the Corvette up to the entrance of the restaurant. He was certainly not expecting to see me—especially behind the wheel—and repeatedly asked, "Why are you here? Why is your Corvette here?!"

The funny thing was, he had just sent me new custom floor mats for the vehicle for my birthday, and I hadn't even taken them out of the boxes yet. All I said to him was "It's yours," as I handed him the keys. He walked around the vehicle in disbelief. Watching his expression and the shock on his face was priceless, and the gratification and significance of that day was the best feeling in the world.

> **That day I felt true intentional success in accomplishing what my wife and I were told we would never be able to accomplish."**

Over the years, my wife and I have personally witnessed a lot of extremely successful entrepreneurs and business owners make a lot of money, only to end up losing it with nothing to show for it at the end.

Something my wife and I have learned over the years is to stay grounded and never live beyond your means—regardless of your financial success.

For us, part of this was based on learning from mistakes we had made previously: having setbacks early on from previous businesses and almost losing everything. After the struggles we faced to get back on our feet, we vowed to do everything we could in order to never go back down that same road again.

It's easy to be tempted to buy a bigger home or even multiple homes; purchase more expensive cars or boats; have more toys, or belong to the local country club just because all of your friends do.

I'm not saying it's wrong to enjoy your successes in life, but I would challenge you to be cautious about overspending and taking on more debt that you cannot afford to pay off comfortably.

> **True intentional success allows you to live your life *debt-free*, not forever in debt."**

When I bought the 50th Anniversary Corvette in 2003, there were only two available between Oregon and Washington. Once I verified the location of one of the two within driving distance of our home, I drove to the dealership. The Corvette was in their showroom. I entered the showroom and proceeded to sit in the car as a salesman quickly came up to me asking "Would you like to drive it?" I responded by saying, "Yes, I'd like to drive it home today."

When he asked about financing, I responded that I would be paying cash.

You see, that Corvette was something I had been looking to purchase for over a year because it was unique—there was a limited number made for that specific model. It was my reward for accomplishing a specific goal that my wife and I had achieved.

One thing that we have always done is set goals with rewards based on success, as opposed to instant gratification.

This is called delayed gratification:

> **Delayed gratification, or deferred gratification, is the ability to resist the temptation for an immediate reward and wait for a later reward."**

Today's society is about instant gratification. You see something in a commercial, online or at the store and buy it without thinking twice. We are all do this—I am no exception, especially for the smaller, less costly items and impulse buys.

As you get older, monetary things are not as important as spending quality time with your family. My wife and I are looking forward to spending more time with our kids, their spouses, and our grandchildren.

As you achieve success, it's also extremely important to plan for your retirement, regardless of your age. Invest wisely, know that it's okay to be frugal, and don't get caught up in what others are doing. Lastly, create multiple streams of income through both your business and in your investments.

> **"Never stop learning regardless of your age, because life never stops teaching."**

As my parents reached their mid-80s, their health started to deteriorate. My mom was diagnosed with dementia and my dad with Alzheimer's disease. The success of our business allowed me to fly up north and spend quality time with both of them on a consistent basis. One day, after my mom passed away, I was sitting with my dad while he was eating breakfast. I took a video of him as I asked the question, "What do you consider success to be in life?"

As I have mentioned before, my dad worked for the same company for over 40 years. My parents were frugal but lived a generous and selfless life. When my dad retired, he was in his mid-60s. He invested well with the company he worked for, and they always lived a debt-free life. After retiring, they lived in Ohio for a portion of the year and in Florida during the winter months. Because of his investments, they enjoyed life, traveled and spent time visiting their four children and grandchildren.

My dad's response to my question embodied who he was, how he lived his life and the impact he had on those around him:

> "Be kind to everyone, help others, be
> yourself, don't be selfish, be outgoing
> (as it's tough for some people to
> do that) and don't get greedy."

His comment didn't surprise me a bit. He lived a life that was a true success and left a legacy that I can only aspire to leave. A year after filming that video, my dad passed away. I wish my mom and dad were still here to read or listen to the words I have written and know that their teaching, example, and guidance were paramount in who I am today.

I recently asked a good friend of mine, who empowers and motivates audiences all over the world, the same question I asked my dad: " What is your definition of success?"

My friend has faced many challenges throughout his life but has never let those trials steal his success. He takes his adversities head on and never uses them as an excuse. He is an incredible motivational speaker, mentor, coach, and author today.

This is what my friend, Roger Crawford had to say:

> I believe true success is found in a life of significance instead of prominence. Often, success is measured by status, wealth, and prestige. As a result, success is all about us and totally self-focused. The definition of prominence is the state of being important or famous.
>
> Of course, with success will come prominence; however, that is not the driving force for high achievers. They

determine success by contribution, value, and impacting others.

Therefore, success is less about us and focused on how we can make a difference.

You said at breakfast, 'My greatest joy is helping other people be successful.' That is significance!

Definition of significance is meaning, substance, and magnitude.

Finally, prominence is fleeting and can be gone in an instant. Significance is sustainable in good and challenging times."

-Roger Crawford
Hall of Fame Speaker and Author

For those of you who do not know Roger Crawford, this is what Sports Illustrated said: *"Roger Crawford is one of the most accomplished, physically challenged athletes in the world! Roger discovered not only how to compete, but also how to win against able-bodied athletes!"* Roger was born with four impaired limbs, but don't tell him that because I think he has forgotten!

Roger's answer to my question was spot on! Our intentional success is measured by the number of lives we have impacted, not the amount of money we've made, businesses we've owned, or cars we've been able to buy.

If our lives are not affecting the people around us, we are not truly successful.

Have you ever asked yourself who is in your sphere of influence? We all have one whether we recognize it or not.

What are you doing within that sphere of influence?

Have you purposed to use the experience you have gained to help others, to encourage them and help them succeed?

Zig Ziglar said it best:

> **You can have everything in life that you want, if you will just help enough other people get what they want"**

Remember we are all leaders and impacting others, even if we don't realize it; whether positively or negatively!

If you are running a business with your spouse, know that people are watching you even more closely than other leaders or business owners; watching how you treat each other, talk to each other; how you lift up and encourage your family.

As we've journeyed through this book together, my wife and I hope you've found valuable insight and have been able to take something away from this book, allowing you to win big in business AND in your personal life.

But more than that, we hope that our story has helped you to believe that anything is possible when you have the right plan in place.

Dream BIG, chase after your goals and inspire others along the way with true intentional success.

ABOUT THE AUTHOR

AUTHOR. KEYNOTE SPEAKER. COACH. ENTREPRENEUR. BUSINESS LEADER.

BRAD TAYLOR HAS a purpose and passion for business, sharing over 40 years of experience, 25 dedicated to serving the real estate industry. Immersing himself in innovative strategies to create awesome results for small businesses, he guides individuals and organizations towards achieving their ultimate goals. With formidable insight into the challenges and opportunities that come from making mistakes and overcoming them, Brad and his wife, Cathy, share their motivational wisdom about taking a risk and owning it. Using "12 Intangibles," they introduce their platform for inspiring others with their belief in Intentional Success.

To contact Brad, go to TheBradTaylor.com